Delight Wier's
Kitchen

By Delight Wier

Library of Congress Catalog No. 79-63288
ISBN 0-87069-283-6

Design by Marilyn Pardekooper

Published by

Wallace-Homestead Book Company
1912 Grand Avenue
Des Moines, Iowa 50309

*Recipe Verse**

*I didn't have potatoes
So I substituted rice;
I didn't have paprika
So I used another spice.*

*I didn't have tomato sauce,
I used tomato paste;
A whole can, not a half can,
I don't believe in waste.*

*A friend said "you couldn't beat it,"
Is there something wrong with her?
I couldn't even eat it;
Would you like to have my share?*

*An old friend, Rhea Young, got wind of my recipe book and contributed this poem.

Contents

Introduction

This book needs a special introduction because it is like no other cookbook. The old saying that the way to a man's (or a family's) heart is through the stomach has in this book been given a new dimension. Delight Wier is fond of saying that her kitchen is the nerve center of the farm and of family life. The food recipes set forth here are not just dishes to feed a hungry husband and children, plus a stream of guests and friends in the home and in countless community "potlucks."

This book is full of many kinds of nourishment, not only for the body, but the soul, intellect, family, and community life. It is dedicated to the enhancement of God's whole Creation, including the human beings who have been given many exciting responsibilities in the creation.

Delight Wier could not have written it any other way. My editorial sense of orderliness rebelled at first against mixing recipes with philosophy, family history, and the comings and goings of a very remarkable family. But I changed my mind. After all, these farm oriented recipes have deep roots in the past. The flavor of the food has to be inextricably mixed with the flavor of people and events that have marched down through the generations.

This farm kitchen is just one step removed from the farm garden and food plants growing wild. The food has a special goodness because it has stood the test of a busy housewife, with little children tugging at her apron strings, getting nourishing dishes ready for hungry workers coming in from the fields.

As columnist for *Prairie Farmer*, Delight Wier has acquired a large following of loyal readers. Her homey mixture of family and food and philosophy, laced with her own special kind of Christian faith, has endeared her to readers and listeners in several states. This book is to be read, not just nibbled at. You will appreciate the food all the more if you also know about the sources from which the recipes came, and the zest with which the dishes have been prepared and enjoyed.

As editor of *Prairie Farmer* magazine, I first met Delight in the offices of the rural department of the National Lutheran Council of Chicago, where she worked as a secretary and preparer of materials for use by churches. She buttonholed me one day when I was visiting that office and asked if I could give her some advice about writing and marketing her product. I have always been a sucker for a pretty girl with a writing gleam in her eye, so I asked her if I could see some samples of her writing. She "just happened to have on hand" an essay entitled "Why I Want to Marry a Farmer" which I took home to study at my leisure.

The central idea of the article was excellent, sincerity was there in abundance, but the style was flat and what we editors call too Sunday schoolish. I relayed my reactions to Delight and suggested she rewrite the article and submit it to one or two of the more prestigous agricultural magazines.

Some months later she reported that the story had been rejected by both magazines. I suggested rewriting it again and said we would use it in *Prairie Farmer*. I was so intrigued by the subject that I started the story on the front page (in those days *Prairie Farmer* did not have full-page color covers) and waited with crossed fingers. The reaction was quick and decisive. There were any number of proposals of marriage from rich old bachelors, but the chief theme of the letters was that this girl was much too starry-eyed and naive. The life of a farmer's wife, the correspondents said, would bring drudgery, disillusionment, and add up to much hardship.

I published some of the pessimistic letters, as well as complimentary ones. Wham! Back came another surge of letters declaring that this young girl was not wrong, that her idealistic view of farm life was real, and that the myth of farm drudgery has been greatly exaggerated. The battle in the "Readers Say" department of *Prairie Farmer* raged for months. As editor I sat back and enjoyed the controversy between the idealists and the pessimists. There is nothing an editor likes better than a lively battle in the letters department. The editor of one of the national farm papers told me later in confidence that the stupidest thing he ever did was to turn down that manuscript.

Well, the Chicago secretary, who had been raised on an Indiana farm and knew more about farm life than the *Prairie Farmer* correspondents had given her credit for, did marry her farmer. He was a young farm lad from west-central Illinois named Ralph Wier, who definitely was not one of the men who proposed to her through *Prairie Farmer.* You will find the story elsewhere in this book.

Some years later I got a letter from Delight Wier asking if she could have a try at writing a column for *Prairie Farmer.* I drove out to the farm and discovered a young couple struggling hard to make a living. To complicate matters, there was a ladylike toddler named Rebecca and twin boys, Danny and David, whom I later came to think of as the "bear cubs." The Wier kitchen was already the nerve center of the farm. Even in the midst of her strenuous life, Delight had not lost the itch to write. So we set about creating the column which became known as a "Letter from a Farmer's Wife." It took some doing. I wanted an earthy, family-farm-centered column. Delight wanted to teach Sunday school. I never succeeded in knocking the Sunday schoolishness out of her writing, and now I am glad of it. It belongs. Anyway, the column grew in quality and influence.

During those hectic sessions by the Wier dining room table, struggling with writing style and content, I got to know husband Ralph much better. He was a hard working farmer, deeply involved in science and management and mechanization. But he also had a quiet, spiritual side that complemented Delight's spirituality in a remarkable way. I recall that whenever I arrived at the Wier farm for one of those sessions devoted to the improvement of the column, Ralph would leave the smoking tractor in the field and come in the house to sit and listen. He would sit in a rocking chair weaving one of those potholders made out of castoff nylon stockings. When the session was over and I went out to the car followed by Delight and the train of little ones, Ralph would hand me that potholder as a gift for my wife Eveline.

As the *Prairie Farmer* column improved and the years passed, that parade of Wiers seeing me out to the car became longer. Timothy arrived soon after the twins, then Maryanne, a fairylike little redhead of whom I was especially fond. Then came Paul and all of eight years later, Jonathan, who was what on the farm we used to call a fall chick. When Paul was christened I had the momentary pleasant thought that he was named after me, but then I noted the march of biblical names working its way down through the Wier tribe, and I readily yielded to the Great Apostle.

Tragedy has had its part in the growth of Delight Wier as a mother-writer. It was a great shock to me when I heard—a day or so after the funeral—that sturdy little Danny had been killed in a farm accident. Sensing the depth of the blow, I once more climbed into my battered *Prairie Farmer* company car and drove out to the Wier farm. I knew somehow that writing that first column

9

after the tragedy would be just about the hardest thing that Delight would ever do. I found the family crushed, of course, and Delight harboring the idea that she must never write another word for publication. Editing can sometimes be a cruel responsibility. I told Delight to put any notion of quitting out of her head. So we sat down once more at that dining room table and I helped her put the story on paper. It was a subdued, almost matter of fact column, with grief held in check. The tens of thousands of parents who read that column in *Prairie Farmer* sensed the hurt that lay under the words.

I count that day with the Wiers the most important in a lifetime of editing. Delight would continue to write and grow better at it. Some years later when the lovely Maryanne also lost her life in an accident, I grieved with the family but I didn't worry. I knew the Wiers would be able to cope.

Ralph and Delight are now grandparents. David is farming with his father. The four oldest are married, which has had the effect of enlarging and enriching a grand family. The wooded hills on that part of the farm near the Illinois River have many ponds, built by Ralph with his trusty bulldozer and lovingly planted by the family with the advice of soil conservation specialists. There is a camp at one of them for crippled and disadvantaged children, created in honor of Danny and Maryanne. Scores, even hundreds of children and young people have been made welcome at the Wier home: the lame and the halt, the bruised and the disadvantaged, lonely foreign students, displaced persons from ravaged countries. Food for body and soul have been dispensed with zest and loving care.

Delight has emerged as one of the best writers of her time. Her writings are now in book form. Her ideas have matured along with her kitchen recipes. She is in demand as a lecturer on family life, environmental concerns, and religious faith. She has done both writing and speaking for the American Bible Society.

Ralph and Delight both grew up in stimulating and enriching homes. The two streams of human experience and excellence coming down from early American history were merged into a family life that has been something special for our time. Religion was a strong ingredient of these lives all the way from pioneer days to the present. Religious faith was a foundation stone in the Wier marriage and it has deepened and grown with the joys, tragedies, and hard work of their married years. So you can expect to find a strong religious vein in this book and a vigorous espousal of the worth of the American home with mother and mother's kitchen as the center.

I can also testify that there is good, wholesome food in those recipes, for I have sat often at the dining room table in that old farmhouse and I have been nourished in body and soul. So good reading! And good eating!

PAUL C. JOHNSON
Editor emeritus, *Prairie Farmer*

Prologue

Prologue

While there's a pumpkin pie in the oven and beef stew simmering on the stove, I'll write a few lines about the old saying that the way to a man's heart is through his stomach. How you treat him in the kitchen is as important as how you treat him in the bedroom. I have grapes in the collander to get ready for jam, but, right now I'd like to share a few thoughts about what contributes most to the well-being of a family.

The farm appears to have a deceptively slow and erratic pace. The truth is that many times throughout the year we could have had cases of nerves because the weather dictates our work. We have learned to take the simple approach of doing first things first so that what counts most gets done. Not one of the demands is more important than feeding the family.

Our home is a busy place at mealtimes. During the summer Ralph has reinstituted the old custom of washing for meals outdoors. He and the men are usually dusty, greasy, and grimy. The small lavoratory in the house is not large enough for men and boys who like to splash the water over face and arms. So Ralph put a stand by the hydrant in the backyard. The last few summers we have outfitted it with a washbasin, soap, and towels.

The water is heated by solar energy in a large plastic container filled after every washing and allowed to sit in the sun to heat for the next mealtime washup. The men hang their towels to dry on the clothesline right by the stand. It's a great energy and labor saving device, besides being long on thoughtfulness on the part of the men. I can start putting out food and having it ready from the time I hear them coming to the time they are washed and in the house.

I like to be on hand when our thirteen-year-old gets off the bus to hear firsthand what is on his mind while he is getting his after school snack. I like to have the coffee hot in case Ralph comes in from the field because of a broken implement. It can save a case of ulcers if I sympathize and make myself available to get the needed repairs.

There's more love dispensed to the family in my kitchen than anywhere else. We women are well equipped to love those with whom we come in contact. There's good food, an optimistic spirit, friendly surroundings, and a listening ear. Psychologists call it ministering to people's needs. In a home kitchen it just comes naturally.

Jonathan, Ralph, and I meet once again at the kitchen table for a hearty supper and a lively exchange of the day's events.

More important questions are settled at family conferences around the meal table than in any other place. Often there's debate or intelligent reasoning, and we hie ourselves to an encyclopedia, dictionary, or recent magazine article to back up a statement. If I don't feed and nurture my family, someone else will. Manners and morals are absorbed along with food. Better sex education is taught at home than by any textbook ever published. Good family relations are demonstrated to a child when Dad comes into the kitchen and pats Mom while looking over her shoulder into the stewpot.

We serve up our meals with prayer to put our hearts right. When the Lord is at the head of our table, father's advice or mother's admonitions go down better.

My meals are plain and practical. Plenty of protein, roughage, and a little sweet treat to top it off. In our affluence we Americans got so far away from good plain food that all kinds of food fads have hit the kitchen. Today there is much talk about soul food. That's what I've been cooking all along. Advocates of soul food create a spell by cooking things like jowls and greens. Any good farmer's wife knows that lots of the greens that grow in fence corners are edible and full of vitamins and iron. Mother used to call them brain food.

Our forebears opened their homes to anyone who passed by. They were doing what comes naturally, sharing bed and board. Maybe we'd better get back to basics. A lot of people go through our kitchen in a year. They come as hired men, visitors, salesmen, friends, and family, but they all come hungry.

Consider yourself fortunate to have someone with whom to share your kitchen. The everyday possibilities at our house offer enough variety to challenge a good cook. Whoever said cooking is drudgery because it's so daily? The variety of demands on a homemaker calls for an exceptionally well trained and responsive woman. Make plans, build your image, make up for the burnt offerings that you have served. There's always another chance to cook. Thank God it is daily.

When there is a soaking rain in the valley it can chill you to the bone. When there are high winds blowing over the prairie it can be lonesome. In the midst of a blizzard the warmth of home is vital. Make the most of your advantages, girls. Even in a heat wave the shade of the porch is like an oasis in the desert. Our families need us. What becomes of them is up to us. Like Esau in the Bible, they may feel like selling their souls for a mess of pottage. We want to be right there serving up what is best for them because these are the people we love.

Part I

Salads, Soups, Stews

I have always liked to cook. That is probably why we have had so many people in our home. Or it could have been the other way around; we invited so many people into our home that I learned how to cook out of sheer necessity.

I started like all brides, with a clean cookbook in one hand and a stirring spoon in the other. However, five children under five put a stop to that. Did you ever see a mother with a nice clean cookbook try to use it with five inquisitive youngsters flocking around? My cookbooks are thoroughly fingered. I have the page yet where Maryanne spilled batter on the banana nutbread recipe when she was learning to make it for 4-H club.

Many beaters for the electric mixer have been ruined. So many crocks were dropped that we changed to aluminum milk pitchers, stainless steel mixing bowls, and iron utensils. On occasion the jelly making kettle has boiled over, the cake has scorched, the bread refused to rise properly, or the jelly roll didn't hold its jelly, but we do have a family of children who know how to cook.

I've never been efficient enough to cover each recipe card with plastic as Rebecca had done prior to the birth of her first child, Andrew. I've never been orderly enough to plan meals for a week in advance because I couldn't know what would get ripe or need picking in the garden. I do know my home economics, vitamins, minerals, and the whole bit about the basic four that everyone needs for good nutrition. I've been in Homemaker's Club for over twenty years. That's the equivalent of a college degree in home economics.

Our kids got plenty of fresh minerals right out in the garden, pulling up half-grown carrots and yelling "What's up, Doc" while eating them. Gardening has been my bane and my blessing, but putting up with it year after year has paid off. Our family members will know how to keep themselves alive on their patches of ground when that time comes.

When the twins were babies some of the garden went to seed and some went to weeds but there was still enough to can and feed the family. Popcorn was a treat, but the children learned that planting, tending, and husking came before eating. Fine, ripe tomatoes need careful watering and weeding before their goodness may be enjoyed. Apple trees must be sprayed at the right time to have disease-free fruit. Even onions need to be dried properly when they are harvested.

I've not had much help in strawberry growing, but I always have help for green bean picking. Their bonus was to eat green beans as they worked. Sweet corn on the cob from the freezer is the big treat in wintertime, but our boys and girls know it must be husked and gathered on the hottest day of the year, not to mention the hot kitchen when it's being canned or blanched for freezing. Then there were those late night wrapping parties. Sweet corn couldn't stand unfrozen overnight.

When the editor asked me to put recipes in my book I looked at him and thought, that is for experts. My degree was in music and art. However, the longer I thought about it, the surer I was that I could at least give some hints on what not to do.

Take baking powder biscuits, for example. I could never improve on the basic recipe everyone uses, but over the years I have learned why I had flat, hard ones that could be bounced. I was putting too much shortening into them and they were heavy. Sad biscuits can't raise.

You can tell on the bread board if your biscuits will raise by the light feel of the dough. Then Rebecca started making biscuits and I saw how she kneaded, shaped, and patted them to death. That is another rule. Handle them fast, cut them quickly, and put them in a hot oven.

Aunt Lessie of my column is a dear friend but not a relative. She lives in southern Illinois and we see her as often as possible. She writes words of advice to us and keeps up to date on our family. She is irrepressible and full of fun. Her "trademark" is to settle on the piano

Lessie Johnson of Jerseyville, Illinois, is the "Aunt Lessie" mentioned frequently in my column. We've been good friends since we served together on the Illinois Farm Bureau State Women's Committee before twins Danny and David were born.

bench and strike up "When the Saints Come Marching Home." People regard her as an outstanding person and wonder at her abundant energy and quick smile.

Since her husband's death several years ago, music is the joy in her life. Her faith is strong and she likes to share it. She recommends that children memorize poems and Bible verses. They are a shield in years to come. Memory is her most valuable possession. What a shame every child cannot have the same Christian home life she has had, with laughter, sunshine, love, and compassion for neighbors.

Her philosophy is that if Jesus seems too far away, it is you who have moved. Christ is waiting where you left him.

I have asked her for some of her recipes. Depend on Aunt Lessie to come up with some of the most practical and yet some of the most unusual recipes I have. There always seems to be a surplus of pumpkins, so I want to give you this unusual one.

Pumpkin Salad

1½ cups milk
1 cup pumpkin
1 container of whipped topping
1 package instant vanilla pudding
1 teaspoon pumpkin spices

Mix the instant pudding with milk and pumpkin. Add spices, then the whipped topping and it's ready to serve unless you want to put it in a pie shell. It is a no-cook recipe.

Geneva Evans likes shortcuts to good eating and gave me this recipe.

Crushed Pineapple Salad

> 1 can crushed pineapple
> 1 large carton Cool Whip
> 1 small size package Jello
> ½ cup chopped nuts

There is no water in this salad. Just put the powder in the pineapple (with juice) and heat, stirring to dissolve Jello. Don't boil. Chill until syrupy. Fold in Cool Whip and nuts. Let set.

❧

If your family enjoys the flavor of sauerkraut you may want to try Stone Jar Sauerkraut in the Canning Section and use it in this recipe.

Kraut Salad

> 1 can kraut, drained
> 1¼ cups sugar
> ¼ cup water
> ½ cup oil
> ½ cup vinegar
> pinch of salt
> small onion, minced
> stick of celery, diced
> red and green pepper,
>   minced

Add minced onion, celery, and red/green peppers to drained kraut. Heat sugar, oil, vinegar, water, and salt to boiling. Pour this over other ingredients and salad is ready for eating. This has come into favor at our community potlucks.

Aunt Murrie brought garden treats for our family every so often. Among them was zucchini squash. Later we started raising them ourselves. My favorite way to serve them is still the recipe I got from her.

Zucchini Salad

Peel squash unless it is very young and tender, in which case the dark green skin looks pretty in the dish. Chop into bite-sized pieces. Add chopped onions and tomatoes. Bits of cauliflower or other vegetables may be used. Mix with salad dressing, salt and pepper to taste.

❦

For the health nuts in the audience I have found a recipe for whole kernel wheat. It is bulging with those vitamins and minerals found in health food stores. I call it Pioneer Salad, but it tastes like potato salad.

Pioneer Salad

2 cups cooked whole kernel wheat
1 small onion, minced
1 stalk celery, diced
3 hard-boiled eggs, chopped
2 teaspoons prepared mustard
¾ cup salad dressing
salt and pepper to taste

Combine ingredients. Cover and chill 2 or 3 hours before serving. Serve on lettuce leaf garnished with sliced tomatoes.

Our family likes plainer salads the best. If it's lettuce from the garden I put salad dressing thinned with vinegar and sugar on the crisp and fresh green leaves. Store-bought lettuce in the winter still comes to the table that way for a crowd, but individually, our boys have three or four kinds of commercial dressings they indulge in. However, I like Lorene McCully's low-calorie dressing with my lettuce.

Low-Calorie French Dressing

Combine in a jar:
1 can cream of tomato soup
½ cup vinegar
⅓ cup sugar
¼ teaspoon celery seed
½ cup salad oil
½ teaspoon salt
⅛ teaspoon pepper

Shake well to mix and chill. Makes 1 pint. Only 46 calories per tablespoon.

Tomato–Green Bean Salad

I learned a lot about good food while I was working in the western states. I stayed at the home of Luberta Jones in the side of a hill one night, and she taught me much. Out there in the sandhills of South Dakota they haven't access to a lot of fresh vegetables, but she had a salad I really liked. She chopped fresh tomatoes, added them to canned grean beans with a little onion and combined it all with salad dressing.

Macaroni-Pea Salad

1 can peas, drained
1 cup cubed cheese
1 cup cooked macaroni
1 cup sweet pickles, chopped
½ cup minced sweet onion
½ cup mayonnaise

Cook macaroni, rinse in cool water. Toss ingredients together and refrigerate. Rebecca likes to take this to potluck dinners. We did just that for the last mother-daughter banquet we attended together. It may have tuna or boiled eggs or cubed ham added for a heavier salad. Young homemakers adapt the old recipes to their diets and tastes.

Casseroles, stews, and soups are favorites in my kitchen. I would never have had the nerve to suggest using leftovers in them—although every cook does—if I hadn't recently read an article in a magazine of high repute. It usually features a page on some gourmet delight that I don't have half the ingredients for and won't go out and buy. But last week the whole article was on making soups and stews out of leftovers. It suggested just the same things that I use when I look in the cupboard and think, "What am I going to have for supper?"

Meat bones, juices, and broths make the base for a hundred varieties of soups. I have been canning a vegetable mixture of beans, tomatoes, onions, cabbage, and carrots from the last of the garden for many years. That quickly gives me what is basic in most soup. Then I look in the refrigerator and find leftovers to toss in also. Don't forget herbs.

Old-fashioned Potato Soup is still a fine warmer-upper on a cold winter day. It is nourishing and satisfying. I like to float chunks of cheese on it. Ralph prefers it more milk than water. This goes for oyster soup, too, so I merely boil the oysters or potatoes in a little water first.

Potato Soup

4 medium potatoes
1 small onion, chopped
1 cup water
salt to flavor (pepper if preferred)
½ cup shredded or chopped cheese
3 cups milk
2 tablespoons butter

Prepare potatoes for soup, cutting them into small squares. Place with chopped onion and seasonings in pan with water to simmer until tender. Add milk slowly while stirring, and warm, do not boil. Float on butter and cheese if wanted. Serve with crackers.

Not only are the varieties of soups almost endless, this one can warm you up or chill you off. Fruit soup can be served as soup or dessert. Now I call *that* versatile.

Fruit Soup

¼ pound dried prunes
1 cup raisins
1 stick cinnamon
1 cup grape juice
1 cup sugar
1 lemon, sliced
1 orange, sliced
4 tablespoons minute tapioca

Wash prunes and raisins and soak an hour or longer in water to cover. Add cinnamon and sugar and cook until fruit is almost done. Add minute tapioca and cook until clear. Remove from stove. Add grape juice, oranges, and lemon. This soup may be varied by adding other fruits. If soup is too thick add more fruit juice. Serve either hot or cold, as a soup or dessert.

Men go for stews better than soup in our family. I can chunk potatoes, carrots, celery, cabbage, and onions for a chicken stew, or I can use green beans, tomatoes, carrots, onions, and potatoes with cubes of beef for our favorite beef stew. I class chicken noodles in the stew category because they, too, are rich and thick. Noodle making was always a big thing for the children because they could get up on chairs and help roll out the dough. When I cut the noodles they liked to help separate the pieces and snatch a few to eat. We made a great deal of fun out of our need for food and family. I use Mom's noodle recipe.

Mom's Noodles

1 egg
1 tablespoon vegetable oil
½ teaspoon salt
1 tablespoon milk
¼ teaspoon baking powder
1 cup flour

Beat egg, stir in oil and milk. Add dry ingredients and form into a ball. Roll out on floured board and dry well. Noodles can then be cut and shaken loose. I usually triple this recipe.

Baked Stew

2 pounds stew meat
1 can (303) tomatoes or
    1½ cups of juice
1 tablespoon sugar
6 small carrots
3 medium potatoes
½ cup diced celery
1 diced onion
3 tablespoons tapioca
1½ teaspoons salt
1 slice of bread, broken

Put all ingredients in a casserole with 1 cup of water poured over the top. Bake covered 3½ hours at 325°. You can adjust vegetables to your own taste. Lois Slager is a busy gal and she says she makes this when she hasn't time to cook.

Chili

1 to 2 pounds ground beef
1 can tomato sauce
1 quart tomato juice
2 cans chili beans
chili powder to taste
onion and garlic salt to taste

Brown ground beef and season with onion and garlic salt; drain off fat. Add other ingredients and simmer one hour or until thick. This is Sandy's recipe which we enjoyed when we were at their house for a Sunday night supper. She served it with lots of celery and carrot sticks. Brownies were dessert.

Ham Beans

A quick old favorite is what Julie calls Ham Beans. Others use beans and pork hocks. They both go well with cornbread, maple syrup, and coleslaw or sauerkraut. It used to be my mother's washday meal. How I looked forward to it. The soup beans used to have to soak overnight to be ready to put with the ham or hocks next morning. Now, I begin about 9 a.m. with ham and beans all in the pressure cooker together without soaking the beans beforehand. When halfway done I open the cooker and add water. The meat may be removed for boning and returned after the beans are done.

It's all ready for the noon meal. Ralph pours maple syrup all over the beans and cornbread. I like to put jam on my cornbread and chili sauce over my beans. I used to use vinegar. Fresh dandelion greens are good with this meal.

Meats, Main Dishes, Home-Curing

I am a connoisseur of fine foods and fancy dishes without claiming that I prepare them. At potlucks there are always those delicious concoctions I like. The ladies say they make them because their men won't have them served at home. That might happen to me if I cooked up fancy things, but the plain fact is that I've never had the time to linger over dishes that took too much time.

My rule of thumb was to have plenty of plain food, meat, potatoes, vegetable, and dessert. The men would come in at noon, eat, and go back to work happy. I've been guilty of putting the plates on the table when they came in for dinner and the food wasn't ready. I might suggest that they look at the newspaper first, but I can't hedge for long. I have to produce a meal somewhere near noon.

Suppertime is fairly regular, but Ralph is guilty at times of not coming in for the meal till it's been held on the back burner and the kids have eaten and are in bed asleep. When that situation arises, I have the choice of going to the garden and weeding one row of vegetables that otherwise might not get weeded, or I can sit down and read that article I didn't know when I'd have time to read. Some wives tell me that they read farm magazines for their husbands and mark articles when he is out in the field moonlighting. I do, too. It is a helpful habit; however, after a long day I'd be more inclined to give myself the treat of reading something I wanted to read. It's surprising how easy it is to become a drudge, and how necessary it is to spend a few minutes a day on yourself.

Since chickens have always been plentiful on our farm, and old hens are usually the ones I select for cooking, the baked chicken recipe can be adapted to use pressure cooked pieces. Our Cambodian family likes this recipe, as they do most other chicken-rice dishes.

Chicken-Rice Casserole

1 chicken
1 cup uncooked rice
1 package powdered onion soup
1 can cream of chicken soup
1 can cream of mushroom soup
2 cans water

Cut up chicken. Place in 9″ x 13″ pan. Sprinkle 1 cup uncooked rice over the chicken. Add 1 can diluted cream of chicken soup and 1 can of diluted cream of mushroom soup. Sprinkle 1 package of powdered onion soup over all and bake at 350° for 1 hour. Can be gently reheated if suppertime is delayed. ~~~

The ladies in our church often serve a chicken casserole for a main dish at a salad luncheon. This one is a favorite.

Chicken Casserole

2 cups diced, cooked chicken
6 or 8 hard-boiled eggs
small jar pimientos (chopped)
1½ cups milk
2 tablespoons butter
½ loaf bread
1 can mushrooms (pieces)
2 cups broth (chicken)
margarine
6 tablespoons flour

Cube the bread and brown in margarine. Make white sauce of milk, butter, flour, and broth. Put layer of bread

31

in buttered casserole, then chicken, sliced eggs, mushrooms, and pimientos. Pour sauce over all and top with bread crumbs. Bake one hour at 350°.

"Make and Bake" Chicken

1 cup fine bread crumbs
1 teaspoon cornstarch
1¾ teaspoons garlic powder
1 teaspoon paprika
1¼ teaspoons salt
1 tablespoon sugar
½ cup flour
1 tablespoon plus 2 teaspoons of oil
1 teaspoon pepper
1¾ teaspoons poultry seasoning
1¾ teaspoons onion powder

When mixed it makes enough coating for 2 chickens cut up. Bake coated pieces covered for ½ hour and then remove cover and finish baking ½ hour at 350°. Betty Ulrick gave Rebecca this unusual coating for baked chicken. The spices give the chicken a zestful flavor.

Chicken Yummy

1 package cooked regular Creamettes,
    seasoned according to package
1 cup chopped pimiento
1 can cream of mushroom soup
4 breasts of chicken
parsley, chopped
1 cup mushrooms (pieces)
2 tablespoons dehydrated (or fresh) onions
½ cup chicken broth
1 cup cheddar cheese
pepper, to taste

If you do not have Creamettes, regular macaroni can be prepared. Add the other ingredients, adjusting the amount of onion if fresh. Pour into buttered casserole and top with chopped parsley. Be sure there is enough moisture, adding more if necessary. Bake at 350°, 45 minutes. This is a good recipe for leftover chicken. We like dark meat, too, so I sometimes add both.

The school of hard knocks teaches many things but it doesn't always stress them in order. I came from a farm family who had a butchering day in the winter and fried down sausages packed in lard. There were also hams cured in brine and some fresh meat. We usually bought a quarter of beef that hung in a cold room. If a warm spell came, Mother had to can the rest of it. What a delicacy canned beef is! I know people who still can part of their beef just for the flavor. When I married and came to this big farmstead where beef and pork hung in the locker to be cut up for our use, I had to decide quickly what cuts of meat I wanted and how much of each. That was a big decision. I learned slowly that there were other kinds of beef than chuck roast steamed tender with vegetables. There were also the tender roasts that should be dry roasted, the juices seared in for mouth-watering tenderness.

Because we go to church and teach Sunday school, I have to put our dinner on before we go. Of all the meals, our children call this our

Favorite Sunday Pot Roast

> 4 to 5 pound chuck roast
> 10 medium potatoes
> 10 carrots
> 5 medium onions
> 2 tablespoons shortening
> 4 to 5 tablespoons flour
> 1 teaspoon salt
> ½ teaspoon pepper

In an electric skillet or oven pan melt the shortening and over high heat brown the roast that has been covered with the seasoned flour. After both sides have been browned, reduce heat and place the prepared vegetables over and around the roast, adding more seasoning if you wish. Add 2 to 3 cups of water, cover tightly and reduce heat to simmer. It will be ready when you get home from church, in 2 to 2½ hours. With this a tossed salad of fresh vegetables and a dessert prepared ahead of time makes our meal.

When I cooked the father-son banquet at our church I searched for a recipe that would please men and boys. Lucille Umbarger helped me and gave me this recipe that is delicious.

Ham Loaf

1 pound ground beef
1 pound ground pork
3 cups Rice Krispies
1 pound smoked ham
  (ground)
2 eggs
1 cup tomato juice

Form little individual loaves out of the above ingredients well mixed. Place side-by-side in a baking pan and baste every half hour with the following sauce that has been mixed and brought to a boil.

½ cup vinegar
¾ cup brown sugar
½ cup water
1 teaspoon dry mustard

Bake at 350° for 1 hour, or 325° for 1½ hours.

Another old standby that can feed a crowd or just the family is Cock-a-Doodle Doo. You might be surprised to know that there is no chicken in it.

Cock-a-Doodle Doo

1 pound hamburger
3 cups cooked macaroni
2 medium onions, chopped
2 cups tomatoes
1 cup chopped cheese or cheese food
½ teaspoon salt
pepper to taste

Brown the hamburger and add onions. Season with salt and pepper, maybe a dash of oregano. Layer the hamburger mixture with the macaroni and tomatoes in a greased casserole. Top with cheese and bake at 350° for ½ hour.

Smoked Turkey

1 12- to 15-pound turkey, fresh or frozen
1 scant cup salt
2 cups Morton's Tender Quick
10 tablespoons liquid smoke
2 gallons cold water

If frozen, thaw bird completely. Place bird neck up in large plastic bucket. Pour brine over bird. Cover and place in refrigerator for 24 hours. Wash well in cold water. Tie wings securely. Dry skin with paper towels. Rub skin with vegetable oil. Place on roasting rack in pan, breast down. Place in preheated 350° oven and brown for 1 hour. Reduce temperature to 250°; tent with foil and bake for 12 hours. Do not undercook. Corrine Gregory, a *Prairie Farmer–Wallaces Farmer* reader, sent me this recipe for a Christmas present.

Baked Lasagna

1 pound sausage or ground beef
1 clove garlic, minced
1 tablespoon parsley flakes
1 tablespoon basil
1½ teaspoons salt
2 cups tomatoes
2 6-ounce cans tomato paste
10 ounces lasagna noodles
5 cups cottage cheese
2 beaten eggs
2 teaspoons salt
½ teaspoon pepper
2 tablespoons parsley flakes
½ cup Parmesan cheese
1 pound Mozzarella cheese,
    sliced thin

Brown meat; spoon off fat. Add next 6 ingredients; simmer 30 minutes. Cook noodles, drain, rinse in cold water. Combine cottage cheese, eggs, seasonings, and Parmesan cheese. Place ⅓ noodles in 13″ x 9″ x 2″ baking dish. Spread ⅓ cottage cheese mixture over. Add Mozzarella cheese, add ⅓ meat sauce. Repeat layers. Bake at 375° for 30 minutes. Let stand 10 to 15 minutes before cutting. Serves 12. Nancy's mother, Donna Johnson, gave me this recipe for family get-togethers. I like Italian foods, and this must be the richest.

Hamburger-Zucchini Bake

1½ pounds hamburger
1 large onion, chopped
2 cups chopped zucchini
2 teaspoons tapioca
½ teaspoon basil
½ teaspoon oregano
3 cups tomato soup or sauce
1 cup chopped Velveeta cheese
salt and pepper to taste

Brown hamburger with onion. Drain fat and add remaining ingredients. Pour into greased casserole. Save some of the cheese for a topping. Bake in a 325° oven for 1¼ hours. Doris Lock is always trying to find uses for her garden surplus, and this uses zucchini squash.

❦

Mary Kennemer was the first to share this rich casserole with me. Since then I have eaten it other places.

Tuna Casserole

1 tablespoon butter
1 cup chopped celery
¼ cup chopped onion
2 tablespoons chopped green pepper
1 can tuna fish
1 can cream of mushroom soup
¼ cup milk
¼ cup water
⅛ teaspoon pepper
½ can chow mein noodles
¾ cup salted cashews

Preheat oven at 350° while sauteing celery, onion, and green pepper in butter. Combine all ingredients; reserve ¼ cup noodles for topping. Pour into ungreased 1½-quart casserole and sprinkle with remaining noodles. Bake uncovered for 30 minutes. Eat and enjoy.

Alan's Macaroni and Cheese

1 box macaroni
5 slices cheese
milk and margarine

Alan Evans wanted me to put his recipe in my book. I told him how my boys cooked when they were first graders, too.

Cook macaroni in salted water as directed on the package. Drain and place back on the stove with some milk and a hunk of margarine. Tear cheese into small pieces over macaroni on very low heat. Serve immediately. Very good for small boys and girls.

Chop Suey Chow Mein

1 pound hamburger
½ cup rice
1 cup chopped onion
1 cup chopped celery
¼ cup soy sauce
1 can cream of chicken soup
1 can cream of celery soup
   (or mushroom)
2 cans water

Brown hamburger and place in a 3-quart baking dish. Add other ingredients and stir to mix evenly. Bake covered one hour at 300°. Uncover and sprinkle with chow mein noodles and continue baking for 15 minutes.

Butchering day on the farm has always been a big day in my life. When I was a little girl it meant going to the neighbors' after school for supper, and afterward everybody played games like "The Prince of Wales Has Lost His Hat." It was family fun with moms and dads playing right along in the circle.

On our own farm Dad had to butcher on a Saturday because he was a teacher, so we had the whole glorious day to watch the grown-ups. The year I was old enough to sit with the women and scrape the intestines for sausage casings was a big thing for me. They actually trusted me to take a silver knife and help get the casings clean without poking a hole in the tender tissue of the small intestines. They doused them in salt water to finish getting them clean before they used them to stuff sausage.

On butchering day there was always liver for dinner and sausage for supper. We do it the same now on our farm. But, because it was Saturday night when we butchered on our home farm, the neighbors all went home so they could get ready to go to town for groceries. Do you remember when Saturday night was the night farmers always bought groceries?

Funny how things boil right down to a person's philosophy of life. Butchering day is an example. It all began when Ralph decided that we should teach our familly of growing boys how to butcher and cut meat. We instituted butchering day for the last week in February, usually a Saturday. At first it was a small beginning with only the family to help.

Ralph took the helm, patiently explaining each step through the day. We butchered two hogs the night before, dressed them, and hung them up to cool overnight. Next morning, after chores, we cut up the meat, shaping hams, loins, saving a lot of meat for sausage. That had to be cut in small pieces and ground. The fat was also cut in chunks. Then there was the lard to render.

I stayed in the kitchen and cooked the two big meals that were necessary.

In the following years we have seen butchering day grow to a big event, with teachers, girl friends, boy friends, neighbors, or relatives joining in the activity. Ralph might groan when he rolled out of bed that Saturday morning, but now butchering day is a tradition.

A couple of years ago one of our schoolboys invited his shapely, blonde teacher to come for the event. She went through the work routine with them, cutting sausage meat and lard. By mealtime she was chilled to the bone and she came in to help me get the meal on the table. She was standing by the stove watching me stir corn and turn sausage patties. She said she realized that it must take a lot of my time in the kitchen feeding this large family. I agreed with her. Then I thought about it awhile and said I really didn't know any place I would rather be than right here cooking for my family. I know the kitchen is the heart of the home.

Our teacher became engaged and married a farmer the next Christmas. You have to be careful what you tell these young people.

Speaking of making a dull job light, by the evening of butchering day the sausage in big tubs had been mixed with seasoning and was ready for stuffing into casings. The lard press was converted into a sausage press with a spout for the slippery casings. It was time for our boys to leave to go on their dates for Saturday night, but do you know they could hardly be torn away from stuffing sausage? It was so exciting, seeing the meat slide into the round casings and coil like a cobra into the tub beneath. I knew then that we had a good thing going.

We end up butchering day by wrapping the meat for the freezer and carrying it downstairs. Tired but contented that he has shown his children something worthwhile about this business of living, Ralph goes to bed for a well-earned rest.

After Ralph started home butchering to supply our meats, the job fell to me to cure the pork. There was a time we couldn't find commercial sugar cure so I went to the old-fashioned mixture pioneers used for hams and shoulders.

Sugar Cure for Meats

8 pounds salt
3 pounds brown sugar
3 ounces saltpeter

Use canning salt and mix thoroughly so that the small portion of saltpeter is well distributed. Apply at the rate of 1¼ ounces per pound and use ⅓ of the mix the first day, ⅓ of the mix the third day, and ⅓ the tenth day. Judge how much curing needs to be done by leaving it seven days per inch of thickness. When cure is completed, wash off the excess and wrap meat. I freeze our cured meat, because it may mold.

Bologna

2 pounds lean hamburger
2 tablespoons Morton's Tender Quick salt cure
¼ teaspoon onion powder
1½ teaspoon liquid smoke
1 cup water
⅛ teaspoon salt

Mix all together. Shape into 2 rolls. Wrap in plastic. Refrigerate 24 hours; remove wrap. Bake on broiler rack 35 minutes at 300°. This recipe comes from Hopedale Illinois. Lois Slager sent it to me. It was the first time I'd seen a recipe for bologna.

All the neighbors in my home community made tasty things at butchering time, but when David tasted summer sausage at a dinner in Indiana, he insisted that he wanted to learn to make it. Emmett Gresley is responsible for this recipe.

Summer Sausage

5 pounds lean raw hamburger or other lean
    ground meat
5 rounded teaspoons Morton's Tender Quick salt
2½ teaspoons mustard seed
2½ teaspoons coarse, black pepper
2½ teaspoons garlic powder

Combine ingredients in large enough container to mix well. Put in refrigerator overnight. Next morning mix again and stuff tightly into 2″ x 12″ white muslin bags. Baste bags with liquid smoke every other day for two weeks while they are hanging in a cool room. It will not have to be refrigerated after curing, but should be wrapped to preserve moisture. Can be frozen. We use ¼ part pork sausaage in our batches. The repeated basting with liquid smoke cures the sausage. There is no cooking.

Potatoes, Vegetables, and Eggs

When I look around my kitchen I realize it is not exceptional in any way. It has windows over the sink where I stand and wash dishes and enjoy myself. It is not a big kitchen in modern terms of those ranch-type homes that go on and on from one island to another to the pantry to the dining table. But our kitchen has been large enough for our family and hired help. Great-grandmother had it constructed so that she could keep her hired girls behind the swinging door and serve the food to the men through a sliding panel on the buffet. That has been the goal of our children ever since I told them how the thing operated, but I never seem to have the help to clear the dining table afterwards.

I remember one exceptional night we played Wier Restaurant and every child helped in some way to cook, serve, and clean up the meal. There was a menu to choose from salads to desserts. Rebecca lettered it. The boys were the cooks. Maryanne was the waitress, and such a pretty, giggly girl you never saw, complete with pencil and order pad. The children had a ball; Ralph tolerated it. The game made one cold winter night memorable for everyone. I highly recommend it to families for an unusual recreation, especially with candles on the dining table to add to the festivities.

Our kitchen is the hub of the farm. It has a linoleum floor because I cannot seem to keep the floor from acquiring muddy footprints. I cringe to think of a carpet with the gallons of milk the children have spilt over the years.

Twin high chairs could sit on newspapers, but when the telephone rang there could be that game of tossing food far enough to miss the newspapers.

Ralph has always provided good equipment for the kitchen, anticipating that I needed a blender, 4-slice toaster, stainless steel mixer and other such important utensils before I realized I needed them. He is electrician when a burner on the stove needs replacement. He also is quick to repair the oven unit because he likes his pies, cakes, and cookies.

Since they have grown up, the children have provided other necessities like can openers, coffeemakers, pots, glasses, and dishes. Paul got tired of plastic glasses so now he regularly supplies glasses for my birthday. We break up about one set a year. The kids know there are days I spend eight hours in the kitchen and they want to make them pleasant hours.

Compliments may be too much to hope for, but just to have the whole family flock in and sit down, visit pleasantly, discuss the news, and exchange ideas is reward enough. When they leave smiling, joking, refreshed after grueling hours in the heat or the cold, ready to face the world again, I know that's what cooking and kitchens are for. The cook is never lonely at this house.

One day after I'd had a flop with the gravy for a fried chicken dinner I realized how much of an art there is to making good gravy. Of course, there's cornstarch gravy which looks beautiful, but I wasn't raised on it, nor was my family, so we make flour gravy.

Mother browned the flour in hot fat and proceeded to add the water. If it's done that way, make sure the water is cold and you never leave off stirring until it is combined properly. I got out my gravy shaker recently and went to using it to combine the flour and water so there wouldn't be lumps. When the children made it they thought it could be put together quickly. Consequently they served raw gravy. Gravy must come to a boil to

45

cook the thickening ingredient. Julie, David's wife, and I have gone over the fine points of gravy making these last few months. We grin and wink at each other when the fellows compliment us on the good gravy for their mashed potatoes. Gravy is a delicacy to be treated, not as an afterthought, but as a delicious accompaniment.

Gravy and biscuits are perhaps the commonest, most mundane things I could comment upon. But they are basics, and I wouldn't have you misled. They are important touches. There are thickened and unthickened gravies. They can be made from the juices of any meat or with milk alone. Just lately I am discovering sausage gravy to stretch a meal beyond the number I was expecting.

I am French enough to like spicy foods, but potatoes are a staple in our kitchen to satisfy both Ralph's and my appetite, whether we have a little Irish in us or not. Amelia Wiemer gave us a treat when she fixed her Dessert Mashed Potatoes. She gave me permission to print the recipe.

Dessert Mashed Potatoes

Cook potatoes with salt added until well done. Drain and mash. Add:

    8 ounces cream cheese
    ½ pint dairy sour cream
    2 tablespoons of butter
    milk as needed
    garlic salt to taste

Put in buttered baking dish. Cover with foil and heat slowly until heated through. Our kids go for this rich delicacy, but a small serving satisfies the tastebuds.

Sometimes I use leftover mashed potatoes with an egg, flour, and garlic salt to shape into pancakes and brown in the skillet.

When I lived with Norwegian Donna Lewis in a girl's club in Chicago she brought to me the wonders of Scandinavian cookery. Now, I have a Swedish daughter-in-law, Nancy Johnson Wier, and she speaks lovingly of her Grandma Johnson's potato pancakes. Here is Donna's recipe for Lefse.

Lefse

4 cups riced potatoes
1 teaspoon salt
1 tablespoon lard
1 tablespoon sugar

Mix these ingredients together with enough flour till dough feels like velvet. Roll thin. Bake on moderately hot grill.

Kumla
(potato dumplings)

1 ham shank or pork ribs
½ cup ham or pork broth
6 cups flour (approximately)
4 cups grated raw potatoes
3 teaspoons salt

Boil ham shank or pork ribs for 2 hours. Combine grated raw potatoes, ½ cup ham or pork broth, and salt. Mix with enough flour to make balls stiff enough to handle with hands. Wet hands in water and form balls about the size of a lemon. Drop in ham broth and cook one hour. Serve with meat already cooked.

Our boys as well as our girls can cook. They have often cooked when Ralph and I were gone. They make treat foods like hamburgers with all the extras poured over and piled on a toasted bun. Rebecca has added several items to our file of recipes. She gave me this recipe because she liked Grandma Wier's hot potato salad.

Hot Potato Salad

4 medium-sized potatoes, diced
4 slices bacon
¼ cup finely chopped onion
1 tablespoon flour
1 teaspoon dry mustard
1 teaspoon salt
1 teaspoon sugar
½ cup water
1 egg, beaten
¼ cup vinegar

Cook potatoes in boiling, salted water; drain and dice. Cook bacon; drain and chop. Using 2 tablespoons of bacon fat, cook onion till brown. Blend flour, mustard, salt and sugar with onion; stir in water; boil 2 minutes. Add 2 tablespoons of hot mixture to beaten egg. Stir into rest of mixture; add vinegar and reheat. Pour hot dressing over hot potatoes; mix in bacon. Four servings.

Scalloped Potatoes

½ cup butter
⅓ cup flour
⅓ teaspoon pepper
½ tablespoon salt
2½ cups milk
¼ cup Milnot or cream
¼ pound Velveeta cheese
⅓ cup chopped onion
3½ pints thinly sliced cooked potatoes

Combine first seven ingredients to make a cheese sauce. Pour the sauce over the potatoes and onion arranged in a buttered 9" x 12" baking dish. Bake 35 to 45 minutes at 350°. Doris Lock gets to make this potato dish at potluck dinners whenever Rebecca is planning the menu. She is crazy about her mother-in-law's scalloped potatoes.

❧

My mother and father always gardened and raised every kind of vegetable they liked. In that way I had a liberal education in vegetables and fruits. I still cannot understand anyone who does not like every kind of vegetable and fruit that grows. I have even learned to eat cooked turnips. That occurred when I lived in a girl's club in Chicago and came home starved at night because I couldn't afford to eat lunch if I did have time. I ate everything put on the table, including delicious mashed turnips which the German cook, Wilhemina, prepared. I haven't taught all my family to eat them yet. They aren't that hungry. In fact, there are a few things Ralph will not taste. I detour around them and prepare only a small amount for the half of the family which likes them. I never attempt to disguise them.

Broccoli Casserole

2 packages frozen, chopped broccoli
1 cup cooked rice
8-ounce jar Cheese Whiz
1 can cream of mushroom or celery soup
small jar mushroom pieces
½ cup chopped celery
1 cup water chestnuts
½ cup chopped onion
½ cup milk

Saute onion and celery in butter, add soup and milk. Add rest of ingredients. Bake at 400° for 35 to 40 minutes. Sandy's mom, Lois Slager, made this for Thanksgiving dinner when we first met the family. She makes it for special occasions. It's yummy.

Broccoli-Cauliflower Casserole

1 box frozen cauliflower
1 can undiluted cheddar cheese soup
1 hard-cooked egg
1 box frozen broccoli spears
butter to season vegetables

Cook vegetables as directed on packages and season with butter or margarine. Drain. Place in a buttered dish with cauliflower at one end, broccoli at the other end. Spread soup over top and bake until cheese bubbles (350° approximately 20 minutes). Decorate top of dish with thin slices of hard-cooked egg. Geneva Evans likes this for the family because it combines two vegetables in one process.

Corn Stuffing

2 cups cream style corn
1½ cups whole kernel corn
1 egg, beaten
1 cup soft bread crumbs
¼ cup chopped onion
¼ cup chopped green pepper
2 tablespoons chopped pimiento
1½ teaspoons salt
dash pepper

Combine all ingredients. Fill center of a crown roast of pork or lamb about one hour before meat is done. Any of us who raise pork or lamb can use this stuffing for a flavorful meat dish. Rebecca's mother-in-law raises lambs and served this with lamb at Rebecca's birthday dinner.

Zucchini Casserole

3 to 4 cups chopped zucchini squash
1½ cups grated cheese
1½ cups crushed crackers
½ teaspoon salt
3 beaten eggs
1 cup milk
½ cup grated cheese
½ cup melted butter

Combine ingredients and pour into a buttered baking dish. Bake 1 hour at 350°. The ½ cup grated cheese and the butter make a rich topping that Julie's Grandma Miller adds to make this a favorite at family potlucks.

One-Eyed Sailors

When Rebecca was in scouting she came home with the most remarkable cookout idea. She took our younger children over to Smiling Pond one noon when Ralph was working on another farm and made One-Eyed Sailors for all of us. She buttered slices of white bread and poked a hole in the middle large enough to hold an egg. With the buttered side of the bread down in a small skillet, she proceeded to break the egg and let it fill the hole, sprinkling on salt and pepper. She had a makeshift lid and cooked them according to our tastes, soft or hard. When she flipped them the yolk ran over part of the bread and made a hearty finger food for kids.

Easy Omelet for Two

Grown-up Rebecca sent me this recipe that she uses for herself and Dale. In blender beat 4 eggs, salt and pepper, and ¼ cup milk until frothy. Pour into heated, small iron skillet with melted margarine or butter. Thin slices of American cheese or Canadian bacon laid on is good, too. Cook over medium-low heat until edges begin to dry. Finish under broiler in oven.

Cooking is certainly a joy, but hardly ever is it the sole occupation of most farm wives. They have to be versatile helpers who thrive on the challenge of modern-day farming.

Of all the professions man can engage in, the profession of farming is probably the most uniquely family centered. I call the farm kitchen the command post of the farm. This is because we talk and plan around the kitchen table.

Over and over again at seminars and study classes we are told that the farm wife is the key to the success or failure of any farm operation. Because farming is still basically a family-centered business, the opinion and attitude of the farm wife are vital.

Specialists talk about the farm wife providing the necessary "immediate backup management." This means, girls, that if the hired man doesn't show up and your husband has to go to the field, you have to know where to put the load of lime or into which bin each kind of bulk feed goes.

I also realize that my attitude is vital to the children's enjoyment of their chores. Many a night after school I've gone out with Jonathan and the others to see baby

Through the many years spent raising our family and operating the farm, Ralph and I have probably drunk thousands of cups of coffee during our "board meetings" at the kitchen table.

rabbits, pigs, lambs, and helped feed them. The adventure element remains high only if they have someone with whom to share their enthusiasm.

Experts also say that the farm wife can inspire and instill the confidence necessary for the husband to manage effectively. Let me tell you, it takes bushels of lunches in the field, going to town for machinery parts, and lots of love. Today with tensions and complexities increasing, it requires more than just hard labor to make the farm succeed. If the farmer's wife has a hand in the bookkeeping, understands how markets move up and down, and why money is tight, she will be the girl he thought he married.

Long ago, the liberation movement on the farm enlisted farm wives to work in the fields and make decisions. Now, more than ever, women are found at the wheel of the tractor. Today we farm women are proud to be on the go, understanding the farming business, working right beside our husbands.

How glad I am to be the stabilizing person when times become rocky. If the Lord allows me such a great responsibility I must not fail. I need to read, listen, and be able to boost morale or call the vet in times of trouble. It seems that we are in a risk-oriented industry, so I must be risk-oriented, too. If I can't sleep at night knowing how far we are in debt, chances are Ralph can't either. That's a far cry from what I thought the marriage vows meant when we took them, but times change and we must be ready.

Uncle Paul Johnson, as the kids call him, can be sure I've taken off my rose-colored glasses if I can admit that this beautiful way of life is a risk-oriented industry. But no one can rob me of the rich experience of mixing work and pleasure so that I look on each new day as a challenge.

I remember one day in spring when Ralph wanted me to bring lunch to the field where he was planting corn. The children were in school and I was eager to help the crop planting however I could. When I got there he stopped the tractor at the end of the field and filled it up with seed. Then he took his lunch pail and told me to go a round with the new eight row planter. He had just put a Dickey John on it and I guess he thought that new-fangled electronic device would intrigue me.

As I started across the field the control lights blinked at me. I felt as busy as an organist at a console. After negotiating the turn properly as Ralph had insisted I learn to do if I was going to help plant corn, I started back across the field. One of the lights stopped blinking. The large planter started whistling at me!

Now I have had men whistle at me, but a machine is something else. I knew it meant trouble. I apprehensively drove to the end of the row and told Ralph what was happening. He laughed and said it had been misbehaving, but it was planting just the same. Whew! What a relief. I could see the family all summer pointing to that row of corn Mother planted — or rather didn't plant.

A farmer's wife has to keep abreast of the new machinery and have a nodding acquaintance with it. She must be able to drive to town and ask for a part and know which color it is. My advice is to take the serial numbers or take the whole broken part along if you can get it into the car.

I really shouldn't complain about having a farmer-husband for a partner. I am his receptionist, switchboard operator, private secretary, bookkeeper and consultant. Who would you rather have do the job than yourself? Keep in mind the many wives with husbands in other businesses who depend first on a blonde secretary.

Part II

Cookies, Desserts, Ice Creams

Children love fresh air, sunshine, and activity. They love to be with animals. We all can tell great stories about kids and pets. I laugh when I recall an inner-city girl who visited here a few years ago and asked Ralph if she could see something born. He told her she was in luck because the sows were farrowing.

Up in the hog barn she and her little sister watched the miracle of birth. She rushed down to the house to tell me all the details. Back and forth the girls ran, watching the sow have five baby pigs. They were quite breathless by this time and she panted, "This is even better than a sex movie, Mom!" How right she was.

I still enjoy my livestock chores. I keep chickens and gather eggs every day. It is a kind of gift, to find an egg in the nest. I thank God for these gifts, even the giddy hens who lay them. The very routine of chores gives satisfaction.

People may shout about being liberated from chores. They may heave a big sigh of relief getting away from milking dairy cows, but the need is basic, not confining. The work should be distributed so that everyone shares the chores and each has free time. Too much work makes Jack a dull boy, but too much play will ruin his day.

Farm families mix pleasure with working for their livelihood. On our farm it is the rule rather than the exception. Work is a boon to a person's well-being and disposes of boredom effectively. We have need of our children's help in this farming enterprise. Ralph has even been known to order the boys to go fishing and catch food for supper! It's a great heritage.

Best of all, chores are the discipline which regulates our lives. Everyone needs to care for something living, whether plants or animals. A fresh air walk can make me look at something else besides my housework and make me appreciate a farmer-husband's work. I feel firsthand the weather conditions he's been working in all day long. I know why there's mud on the back porch, grease smeared on the lavatory, and hayseed on the bed pillow. What is that saying about walking in another's moccasins a mile before judging him?

I try never to say "No" to the children when they suggest helping to make cookies. Even if there isn't time before the meal to bake them, they can be placed into the refrigerator for baking afterwards. Children usually think about making cookies around mealtime at our house.

Usually I bake quick cookies, but the children are very patient with rolling out sugar cookies, balling snicker doodles, and cutting pfeffernuss. I make some cookies when no one else is around to help, but the ones I remember are the ones I've had help doing. When Rebecca and Maryanne were home together they went through a time of making a lot of no-bake skillet cookies because they had brothers and a dad to eat them. To this day, Paul still asks for them. Here is a fancy variation.

No-Bake Skillet Cookies

1 6-ounce package semi-sweet chocolate pieces
⅓ cup butter or margarine
1 jar marshmallow cream
½ teaspoon vanilla
1 cup coconut
3 cups rolled oats

Melt first 3 ingredients in a pan, stirring until smooth. Remove from heat. Add vanilla, coconut, and oats. Mix thoroughly. Drop by spoonfuls on waxed paper. Refrigerate. Makes 3 dozen cookies.

❧

I go for the plain cookies and try to leave the high calorie ones for others to make. I have always let my children dip into the cookie jar for cereal cookies that had a lot of chew to them. This doesn't spoil their appetites for supper.

Mother had the best cookies in her cookie jar, whether they were the large round sugar cookies or the oblong butterscotch ones. Daddy dunked them all in his coffee. Grandchildren climbed on chairs beside him and dunked theirs in milk. It's surprising how alike grandkids and grandpas are when it comes to cookie tastes.

Our children expect me to make pfeffernuss and springerli cookies every Christmas season. Rebecca even asked for a springerli rolling pin for her kitchen.

Pfeffernuesse

½ cup light corn syrup
1 cup shortening
⅓ cup water
1 cup sugar
½ cup molasses
2 eggs
6 ⅔ cups sifted cake flour
1 teaspoon soda
¼ teaspoon ground cloves
¼ teaspoon allspice
½ teaspoon nutmeg
1 teaspoon cinnamon
3 tablespoons anise seed

Blend together first 6 ingredients. Add sifted dry ingredients and fold in until stiff dough is formed. Roll into ½" rolls and cut into ½" pieces. Bake at 325° until puffed up and lightly browned. Cool. Shake on powdered sugar.

We chew on hard cookies and have a taste for crunchy ones. I give the children more plain cookies than fruit-filled ones because a long time ago Ralph told Timmy that raisins were bugs. Ever since they have been unpopular in cookies here. Jonathan still has to overcome his dislike for them, too.

Grammy's Butterscotch Cookies

4 cups brown sugar
7 cups flour
4 eggs
1 cup shortening (½ margarine, ½ lard)
1 scant tablespoon cream of tartar
1 scant tablespoon soda
1 scant tablespoon vanilla
1 teaspoon salt

Cream the brown sugar and shortenings with the salt. Add the eggs one by one, mixing in between additions until smooth. Add the flour by the cupful with the cream of tartar, soda, and vanilla. Knead at last on the bread board, with more flour if needed, until well blended and shiny looking. Next divide in about 4 big lumps of dough, roll each lump in a roll 2 inches in diameter. Wrap each cylinder in waxed paper and refrigerate overnight. It can be refrigerated as long as a week.

Heat oven to 375°. Slice each roll into ½" to ¼" rounds; crease cookies with a fork dipped in cold water after each imprint. Brown sugar cookies burn easily, so a close watch will be necessary. Your oven might need close checking for the first couple of pans. To make cookies oval-shaped as the grandchildren like them, press on each roll as you slice it. Easy to make. Grammy is explicit in her directions, bless her heart. I'd have never become a cook if she hadn't been.

Christmas Gems

1½ cups white shortening
3¾ cups white sugar
6 eggs
1 cup dark molasses
5 cups unsifted flour
3 teaspoons soda
3 teaspoons salt
3 teaspoons apple pie spice
6 cups regular rolled oats
1½ cups chopped pecans
3 cups raisins
8 ounces red and green candied cherries
8 ounces candied pineapple

Mix thoroughly first 4 ingredients. Sift together next 4 ingredients. Combine and stir in oatmeal, pecans, raisins, and cherries, chopped fine. The pineapple should also be finely chopped. Bake in lined miniature cupcake pans at 375° for 8 to 10 minutes or until lightly browned. These are best when aged for 10 days or so in freezer. They are so nice for gift-giving or to serve at that special holiday party says a *Prairie Farmer-Wallaces Farmer* reader, Corrine Gregory. She enjoyed my column so she sent this recipe.

Wagon Wheel Cookies

1 package chocolate cake mix
4 tablespoons flour
½ cup cooking oil
2 eggs

Mix ingredients to the right consistency for cookies. Either refrigerate or immediately shape into balls and roll in powdered sugar. Press with a glass to flatten. Bake on ungreased cookie sheets in a 350° oven for 12 minutes.

I have used this same recipe substituting 2 packages of brownie mix. Sandy, my daughter-in-law, and Jennifer helped me with the recipe and the boys proved their worth by taste-testing them when they were cutting wood.

Krumkake

3 well-beaten eggs
½ cup sugar
½ cup melted butter
1 teaspoon lemon extract
½ cup flour

Add sugar to eggs and beat. Add melted butter to mixture, then flour and flavoring. Drop by teaspoons on krumkake iron and bake to a light brown. (When I worked among Scandinavian ranchers and farmers in the northwest states all of these delicious treats were savored with black coffee.)

Fattigmand

4 whole eggs
2 egg yolks
6 tablespoons sugar
6 tablespoons top cream
1/8 teaspoon salt
cardamom seed
1 teaspoon vanilla
flour to roll

Mix all ingredients together and beat lightly. Use lefse rolling pin if available. Fry in deep fat. Cut in diamond shapes before frying.

Pepparkakar Cookies

1½ cups syrup
1 cup shortening
1½ teaspoons soda
½ cup buttermilk
1¼ cups sugar
2 quarts flour
1½ teaspoons cloves
1½ teaspoons ginger
1½ teaspoons cinnamon

Mix in evening and let stand overnight in refrigerator. The next morning, roll out very thin. Bake at 300° about ½ hour until lightly browned. If well hidden these cookies will keep for several months.

Tea Tassies

1 small package cream cheese
¼ pound butter or margarine
1 cup flour
1 egg, slightly beaten
¾ cup brown sugar, packed
½ teaspoon vanilla
½ cup pecans

Mix the first 3 ingredients well with a fork. Make 18 small balls the size of a walnut. Place in greased muffin tins and flatten. Prepare the filling of egg, sugar, vanilla, and pecans and put into each flattened tassie. Bake at 375° for 20 minutes. Cool before removing from pan.

Applesauce Cookies

1 cup sugar
½ cup butter
1 egg
1 cup raisins
1 cup applesauce with 1 teaspoon soda
½ teaspoon cinnamon
½ teaspoon nutmeg
½ teaspoon salt
1 cup nutmeats if desired
2 cups flour

Blend sugar and shortening, beat in applesauce. Add remaining ingredients and beat until blended. Drop onto greased cookie sheet. Bake at 350° for 12 to 15 minutes.

There are always those apples that need to be made into sauce in the fall. This cookie recipe will please the men after the applesauce is all made.

Seven-layer Cookies

1 cup melted butter
1 cup of mashed graham crackers
1 cup coconut
1 can Eagle Brand milk
6 ounces butterscotch bits
6 ounces chocolate bits
1 cup chopped pecans

Layer dry ingredients together in a 12"x9" greased pan. Drizzle butter and Eagle Brand milk over top. Bake 20-25 minutes at 350°. Julie makes these for parties.

Lorene McCully's Rhubarb Crunch

4 cups rhubarb pieces
1 cup sugar
2 tablespoons flour
2 tablespoons butter

Mix these ingredients and let stand in buttered 8" or 9" pan.

Combine:

1 cup sugar
1 teaspoon baking powder
1 large egg, beaten
1 cup sifted flour
¼ teaspoon salt
½ cup oatmeal

Mix until crumbly, place on top of mixture in pan and shake down through rhubarb. Bake 40 minutes at 375°. Apples or peaches work well with this recipe, too. Our family gets apple crisp from this recipe very often. Sliced frozen apples work well. I add cinnamon to them.

When the babies were little and I was feeding them egg yolk in their cereal, I had lots of egg whites to use up. I found that everyone here liked meringue shells. They are easy to make, yet a scrumptious dessert when filled with strawberries and ice cream. This is the same as Schaum Torte.

Meringue Shells

6 egg whites (¾ cup)
2 cups sugar
1½ teaspoons lemon juice

Beat egg whites (room temperature) until stiff. Gradually beat in half of the sugar. Then add lemon juice alternately with the remaining sugar. Vinegar can be substituted for lemon juice. Beat until very stiff and glossy. The individual shells should be dropped by the spoonful on brown paper on a baking sheet. Hollow out a center to hold the ice cream or other filling. Bake at 275° for about 40 minutes. This will serve 12 if they aren't all starving boys in from haymaking. All sorts of ice cream toppings are popular around here for these delicacies.

Cherry Delight

1 package cream cheese (8 ounces)
1 can Eagle Brand milk
½ cup Real Lemon
1 can cherry pie filling
¼ cup margarine
¼ cup sugar
1⅓ cups graham crackers

Crush graham crackers and mix with melted margarine and sugar in the bottom of a 9″ x 13″ pan. This may be baked briefly or it may be used unbaked, according to your time. On this firmly pressed mixture layer the cream cheese, Eagle Brand milk and lemon mixture, which was mixed at room temperature in a small mixer bowl till creamy. Spread cherry pie filling over the top and chill until firm. I use my own frozen cherries cooked in their own juice and thickened with cornstarch and sweetened with my favorite sweetener.

Glorified Rice

4 cups cooked rice, salted
2 tablespoons butter
1 can crushed pineapple
2 cups marshmallows, large or bite size
½ cup chopped pecans

I use leftover rice for this recipe because my mother used it this way. Good reason! However, rice may be boiled. While hot add marshmallows, butter, and pineapple. Stir to melt marshmallows. Then add nuts. Marshmallow creme may be used and will be ready sooner. It may be eaten warm or cold. Refrigerates well and is a good leftover.

Grammy is really an innovator. She searches the magazines and newspaper recipes daily. She loves to serve us something we've never tasted when we come to visit her. Always quick to share the recipe, she is happy to have been the one who passed the treat along to us. This dessert was a novelty to us a few years ago.

Pistachio Pudding Dessert

1 package pistachio pudding mix
1 large can of crushed pineapple
1 6-ounce container whipped cream
1 cup marshmallows
½ cup nutmeats

Stir pineapple and juice into pudding mix. Fold in whipped cream, marshmallows, and nuts. Refrigerate until ready to serve.

Peach Pudding Dessert

1 cup flour
¾ cup granulated sugar
2 teaspoons baking powder
¼ teaspoon salt
½ cup milk
3 tablespoons vegetable oil
1 can sliced peaches, drained
1 cup packed brown sugar
¼ cup finely chopped nuts
1 teaspoon cinnamon
1 cup boiling water

Mix flour, granulated sugar, baking powder, and salt. Beat in milk and oil until smooth. Pour into ungreased baking pan, 8″ x 8″ x 2″. Arrange peaches on top. Mix brown sugar, nuts, and cinnamon; sprinkle over peaches. Pour boiling water on all. Bake until wooden pick inserted in center comes out clean, 60 to 70 minutes, at 350°. Serve with whipped cream if desired. Serves 6 if everybody has just one helping!

Rhubarb Dream Dessert

1 cup flour
5 tablespoons powdered sugar
½ cup butter
2 beaten eggs
1½ cups sugar
¼ cup flour
¾ teaspoon salt
2 cups finely chopped rhubarb

Blend together first 3 ingredients for a crust. Press into an ungreased 7½" x 11" pan and bake at 350° for 15 minutes.

Mix together beaten eggs, sugar, flour, salt, and rhubarb. Spoon into crust and bake for 35 minutes at 350°. Serve warm with whipped cream or plain. This serves six people if they aren't too hungry. You may want to double it. Doris Lock's recipe dresses up everyday pie plant into a fancy dessert. Of course, Ralph prefers it with a big scoop of vanilla ice cream on top.

Fruited Bread Pudding

1 cup bread pieces
2 eggs, beaten
1 teaspoon vanilla
¼ cup sugar
½ cup cooked raisins
2 cups milk
¼ teaspoon salt
1 tablespoon margarine
1½ cups pared, diced apples

Soak bread in milk, add eggs, salt, sugar, and vanilla. Meanwhile simmer apples in a little water. Put half of bread mixture in baking dish, put in apples and raisins, then add rest of mixture. Place dish in pan of hot water. Bake at 325° for one hour. May be dotted with butter and cinnamon.

Ever since the children have been old enough to ask their parents for snow ice cream on a winter evening, the first snowfall has symbolized the beginning of tobogganing, ice skating, cocoa, and snow ice cream parties. It is so simple to gather a big pan of the fluffy white stuff and leave it in a cool place till just before time to eat it. Then

I combine in the blender the eggs, milk, cream, vanilla and lemon flavorings, salt, and sugar. In a jiffy the mixture poured over the pan of snow turns into a delectable dessert. The ingredients are the same as for freezer ice cream but omit the cornstarch. Since the snow melts somewhat, I cut back the milk proportions.

Snow Ice Cream

1 gallon fresh snow
Mix in blender:
4 eggs
1 cup sugar, or less
1 teaspoon salt
1 teaspoon vanilla extract
1 teaspoon lemon extract
1 cup cream
1½ cups milk

Stir into the snow until of consistency desired. Add more snow if necessary.

Oatmeal is a common breakfast at our house in winter. I didn't know there was any other way to eat it except with milk and sugar until black children visiting at our house buttered their bowl of cereal. Then our Scottish IFYE came and showed us how to use boiling water in a bowl of oats and beat it until smooth. They just use salt to season and they called it "bruce." We add raisins to the oatmeal while it is cooking for more iron and good flavor.

After we sold our dairy cows and bought as much as 2 gallons of milk a day, I learned to use powdered milk. We like it because it is non-fat and full of nutrients. We serve lots of it instead of pop and sweetened ades that are hard on teeth and cost more in the long run. Here again choose nature's best. Your body deserves it.

We use a lot of milk desserts. Homemade ice cream used to head the list. Right behind it comes milk shakes. Eggnog also is a favorite. I like to make it because I have eggs from our own flock of chickens. For the work, hens are a great reward. We shower our friends with our fresh country eggs when we have plenty. We inherited Grandma Wier's homemade ice cream recipe and we use it a great deal. It uses lots of eggs.

Grandma's Homemade Ice Cream

2 quarts and 1 cup whole milk
1 tablespoon cornstarch
1½ to 2 cups sugar
6 beaten eggs
2 cups cream
2 tablespoons vanilla
1 tablespoon lemon extract

For one gallon of ice cream in the hand freezer, combine the first 3 ingredients and cook together till mixture coats the spoon. Then slowly add the eggs beaten with a small amount of the cream. Any kind of cream can be used, even vegetable base. I have even used reconstituted powdered milk for this recipe. The richness depends on what goes into it. After the flavorings and cream are added, it can go directly into the freezer without cooling.

When our children were younger we had a family singing group. They sang with more or less enthusiasm, but one number they all put their hearts into was the title song from the movie, *The Sound of Music*. It became our theme song.

Maryanne, Timothy, and I chased away the gloom on a dark, rainy day with a spirited rendition of "O What a Beautiful Morning."

The family tradition lives on! Ralph, Jonathan, and I try a little close harmony of some old favorite songs.

Maryanne and Rebecca would do a duet on the verse and the boys joined in with gusto on the chorus while Ralph held Jonathan in his arms and kept an eye on everyone.

The inspiration for singing this song has come from our own farm. It was not hard for me to come to Illinois to live when Ralph brought me to this old home nestled in a cove among the hills of the "second bottoms" of the Illinois River Valley. I had come to a place of beauty. As he and I rode through the timberland on horse, jeep, or tractor, I learned bit by bit the history of these hills.

The prehistoric Hopewell Indians used to inhabit this territory because of its excellent hunting and fishing possibilities. They ranged all up and down the river valley, camping here and there. Later historic Indians used the same area, absorbing the Hopewellians. Chief Senachewine had gardens across the river from us. We are sure our land saw their tepees. Artifacts are found all around this territory. David uncovered the latest arrowhead while leveling the ground around his new house.

White settlers came around 1832. John Wier migrated from West Virginia because of his desire to free the slaves. He bought the surrounding acres, including our home farm. He built a cabin on the hill above our house by a gnarled mulberry tree. When farming expanded and horses needed to be stabled, the homestead was relocated down the hill at the present site. Many fine horses were housed in the big bank barn, and hired men stayed the year around, cutting wood for furnaces in winter and working crops in summer.

The only remaining original building is the old cider-house standing atop our hill. It is a romantic reminder of a colorful past. The Wier family were orchardists and grew thousands of bushels of fruit. They made cider for farmers miles away and shipped many barrels down the river, bound for cities of the world.

There are clay pits on top of the hill, evidence of the first generation's brickmaking business. Pioneers were resourceful and had to fill the needs of their neighbors as well as their own. We don't know why they saved our beautiful virgin maple timber, when almost to the fence-line neighbors lumbered off their maple for furniture manufacturers. My belief is that they were too "Scotch" to part with them for so little money. They kept them and made some of the sweetest maple syrup in the county, year after year.

When we walk along the creek over to the maple grove I imagined tepees standing on Oak Hill. The children could see them, too. Anyone with a little imagination could envision what I was talking about.

Then we listened to the gurgle of the creek and birds chirping above it. This same creek was running water for the first settlers. Now, we preserve it and leave brush on the adjacent hillsides to stop erosion. We let logs lie where they fall along its bank. We have taken a quail census for several years. Small wildlife like the cover along the creek. Ducks raise their young in the dense multiflora cover there. Rabbits hide and watch us as we walk by.

Ralph learned early to conserve these natural resources, preserving with gratitude what his forefathers saved. Santayana wrote, "Those who do not remember the past are condemned to relive it."

Aldo Leopold said, "The shallow-minded modern who has lost his rootage in the land assumes that he has already discovered what is important."

Soil and Water Conservation District activities have helped to save this precious land. In 1935 Grandpa Wier brought the Veterans of Foreign Wars, tough men for a tough job, to reclaim a ten-acre plot of eroded hills. They built erosion control dams and terraces. Wire, posts, and straw went into the sides of the hills to hold the soil until young trees could take over. In 1938 and 1939 the men reforested thirty acres to locust, evergreens, and multiflora roses. They cut 15,000 posts out of the original locust stand for installation of soil fences around the county. Locust seed was furnished for other plantings.

In 1940 Ralph went to conservation camp and learned more. He made grass waterways and laid out contours. In 1942 he built our first pond. Now we have six.

It wasn't hard to fall in love with this farm as well as this man. He brought me to a five-generation, working family farm.

Since our marriage we have taught each child to love the land. I have always been ready to put the broom down beside the pile of sweepings and go when a child urged me to take him for a walk. Teaching the children to love nature was also one way of not becoming a drudge. I surely must have looked like a mother duck with two or three ducklings trailing along behind when we went to the creek after supper for a nature hunt. Ralph would be out in the field working. We would take brown paper bags and give five points for everything of interest a child could find. We learned what poison ivy, hedge balls, and multiflora rose berries were. Sometimes we saw the creek go dry in summer. That meant no more wading, or water for thirsty animals. I'm sure they will remember their mother saying, "Don't ever waste water," if they don't remember me for anything else.

When they were big enough to go with Ralph they helped him plant evergreen trees. They soon begged to help tap the maple trees and haul sap to the sweet shop. They were hooked. Not only did they like fishing and swimming in ponds, they like working to keep them in shape.

Wintertime saw us build a toboggan hill on the north slope of Saddleback Ridge. They all learned to ice skate on our pond. David took a ten-acre plot of reforested trees, and with the help of the district forester, girdled the undesirable ones to let the maple, walnut, oak and coffee trees grow better.

We joined the Audubon and Nature Club. Maryanne put up several bluebird boxes for her 4-H project. David built wood duck nests and installed them in trees. Tim drew plans and built an erosion control box in 4-H. Ralph tries to keep a hive or two of bees around the place for pollination and for our own honey.

We are concernd about our environment. Eric Sevaried has said, "Earth Day will have to be extended to Earth Year, Earth Decade, yes, Earth Century if poisoning of air and loss of soil is to be appreciably slowed down."

We chisel-plow fields to prevent wind erosion. We could, if necessary, go entirely to liquid organic compounds and use biodegradable soaps in our house. I read an earthy little book that taught herb remedies, organic gardening, and the use of compost pits. There are many ways to simplify life when we can't keep up the rat race anymore.

We also work at rural-urban relations. When a child picks up a beautiful Osage orange fruit, I like to tell him about the reason pioneers brought those gnarled and twisted trees here to hold the soil from eroding and to fence their animals. Living fences they called them. Now the prairie is being denuded of those remarkable trees, the last barriers to wind erosion. Fencerows are gone where birds could have nested and wildlife could have hidden and lived.

We named all our hills. The farms are called unusual names like Stony Lonesome and Buffalo Waller. Ralph continues to renovate pastureland. I recycle paper, tin cans, glass bottles, and write congressmen when they need support for a conservation bill. When we learned that five counties of good Illinois soil have already washed down the river, building up a floodplain in

Louisiana, we urged others to be alert also. Ralph concludes that he wants to leave the land better than he found it. Coming generations deserve all that we can preserve for them.

Pies, Cakes, Breads

Diet conscious, I cook our vegetables as plainly as possible. In homemaker classes I learned that it's the additions to vegetables that give the calories. So, I cook most vegetables in salted water, thickening them only for company meals. I do not even butter them, but the boys do. Our appetites have become simpler from this practice and I believe healthier, too. Those who needn't worry over excess fat or who follow a farmer all over the field all day can have a second helping.

Fruits are best fresh, raw, in their own juice and skin. I am first to admit that I put pies full of fruit into the oven every week in the year. Apple pies, cherry pies, and berry pies run the highest preference and I don't make them any different from the way you do. Maybe I cut down on the sugar so that the men can put a dip of ice cream on top. Ralph dearly likes pie a la mode.

When the children were little, pumpkin pie was one of the first I fed to them. They always ate pumpkin, squash, or even sweet potato pie with the same enthusiasm. If the pie were cold, whipped cream went on top, but most of our pies are eaten warm the first meal.

Everybody knows mother is in a good mood when she makes a cream pie. The time it takes to cook the filling, whip the meringue, and carefully watch the browning is worth it if there's a spare crust waiting to fill. You name it. We like all kinds of pies. In the spring I make a rhubarb cream pie with eggs. I use my blender making pumpkin pie. It combines the ingredients from the pressure-cooked pumpkin in the skin all the way to the cream mixture poured into the shell.

I have several shortcuts. The quickest one when all else fails to give me enough time is Impossible Pie. It makes its own crust.

Delight's Impossible Pie

> 2 cups milk
> 4 eggs
> ¾ cup sugar (or artificial sweetener)
> 1½ teaspoon vanilla
> ¼ cup melted margarine
> ½ cup biscuit mix
> nutmeg

Put all ingredients in blender and mix 3 minutes at medium speed. Grease and flour a 9″ pie pan. Pour into pan and let stand 5 minutes. Shake nutmeg over the top. Bake 30 minutes, or until brown, at 350°.

✦

I usually make apple pie with unpeeled fruit, but mother made the king of apple pies when she didn't have enough apples and added raisins to fill out.

Apple-Raisin Pie

3 cups of sliced apples
½ cup raisins soaked ½ hour in hot water.
  Drain and save liquid.
1½ cups sugar
2 tablespoons flour
½ teaspoon cinnamon

In a bowl place apples, flour, raisins, sugar, and cinnamon. Lightly stir to blend, adding 1 tablespoon of raisin water. Prepare a pastry-lined pan and sprinkle sugar and flour over the bottom. Pile the apple-raisin mixture into pan. Filling should be heaped a little to allow for settling in the baking. Top with vented crust. Bake at 425° for 15 minutes or so, then bake at 350° 35-40 minutes.

Cream Pie

1 carton half-and-half cream
¼ cup cornstarch
¾ cup sugar
salt to taste
½ stick margarine
1 teaspoon vanilla
baked pie shell

Mix all ingredients. Cook slowly until thickened and cornstarch is thoroughly cooked. Take from stove. Pour into baked pie shell. Pour 2 teaspoons melted margarine over top of pie. Sprinkle cinnamon over top and broil 2 minutes. Watch constantly. Julie's Grandma Rhine taught her how to make this delicately flavored goody.

My Mother's Piecrust

4 cups flour
1 tablespoon sugar
1½ teaspoons salt
1½ cups lard
1 egg
1 tablespoon vinegar
½ cup water

Combine dry ingredients. Cut lard through dry mix. Add vinegar to egg and stir with fork. Combine with flour mixture plus ½ cup water. Knead piecrust till easy to shape into a ball. Break off portion to be used and roll out on floured board. Store unused portion in refrigerator.

My Mother's Butterscotch Pie

1½ cups brown sugar
1½ cups water
butter, size of a walnut
3 tablespoons flour
3 eggs, separated
1 baked pie shell, cooled

Add flour to sugar and stir into the water in a pan. Cook until thick and smooth. Beat egg yolks. Stir a little of the hot mixture into the beaten yolks; stir, then add to hot mixture and cook a few minutes; add butter; stir and cool. Pour in pie shell.

Meringue

Beat egg whites until foamy. Add ¼ teaspoon of cream of tartar, continue beating until whites are stiff and able to stand in peaks. Gradually add ¼ teaspoon salt and 4 tablespoons white sugar. Pile on top of filling, bringing out onto piecrust edges. Swirl in peaks. Bake at 325° until golden brown. Makes an 8-inch pie.

When it comes right down to favorite recipes, I must admit I have used everyone else's and liked them so much I haven't perfected many of my own. This maple syrup pie was inspired by Aunt Lessie, who first gave me the approximate ingredients. Ralph encouraged the production of a maple syrup pie because he has always like to tap the trees in early spring and produce his delicious syrup. I had to learn to like the stuff, having had only boiled white and brown sugars for pancakes as a child. Now, I too am addicted. We have a whole family of maple-flavor lovers, and they think it odd that there's a person in the world who doesn't like maple syrup. I use it in custards and baked beans. It goes well in bread pudding and candy.

I use the regular baked custard recipe with 2 table-spoons of maple syrup added in place of part of the sugar for a 6-egg recipe. Nutmeg can be omitted then. I have learned a lot about making creamy custards. They must be baked slowly in a pan of hot water. Overbaking or too much sugar can make them turn watery and separate. I like to take baked custards to potlucks and watch peoples faces light up. Bread pudding can be altered in the same manner, although you might want a little more maple syrup.

Maple Syrup Pie

Aunt Lessie sent me this recipe. It became a favorite of the children.

3 tablespoons cornstarch
4 tablespoons cold water
4 tablespoons maple syrup
⅔ to ¾ cup white sugar
1½ cups hot water
¼ teaspoons salt
2 egg yolks
2 tablespoons butter
baked pie shell

Dissolve cornstarch in cold water. Add this mixture to the maple syrup, sugar, salt, and hot water. Cook, stirring constantly, until thickened and clear. Mix egg yolks with a little of the hot mixture and combine, cooking 3 minutes more. Add butter and cool. Pour into baked pie shell.

❧

Aunt Lessie's Stand Up Meringue topped off Maple Syrup Pie to perfection.

Stand Up Meringue

1 tablespoon corn starch, moistened
½ cup boiling water
2 egg whites
¼ teaspoon salt
2 tablespoons sugar

Moisten corn starch with a small amount cold water. Pour over this ½ cup boiling water. Stir and let cool. Beat egg whites until soft peaks are formed. Gradually add salt, sugar, and cornstarch mixture, beating until stiff peaks are formed. Pile on pie, sealing edges, and brown at 350° 12-15 minutes.

Aunt Lessie's Burnt Sugar Pie

4 tablespoons sugar
1 cup boiling water
1 cup brown or white sugar
2½ tablespoons cornstarch
3 tablespoons cold water
⅛ teaspoon salt
2 tablespoons butter
2 eggs
1 teaspoon vanilla
1 baked pie shell

In a heavy skillet burn 4 tablespoons sugar, the darker the stronger, then dissolve in the boiling water. Add the brown sugar. Dissolve cornstarch in cold water and pour into hot syrup. Let thicken. Beat egg yolks with vanilla and salt and stir into hot mixture. Cool; pour into baked pie shell. Use whites for meringue topping on pie filling after cooled.

Aunt Lessie's Impossible Pie

2 cups milk
1 cup coconut
½ cup flour
¾ cup sugar
4 eggs
1 teaspoon vanilla
¾ stick margarine
¼ teaspoon salt

Her Impossible Pie has a bonus of a cup of coconut. It uses plain flour instead of biscuit mix. Place ingredients in blender and mix. Pour into greased and floured pie pan. Bake at 350° for 45 minutes. This pie forms its own crust as it bakes.

Aunt Florence usually brought her girls out to help our children celebrate their birthdays. She brought an unusually good chocolate cake one time when I had a small baby and especially appreciated the help. From that time on, this cake was looked forward to as a rare treat for birthdays or special times.

Chocolate Cake

2 squares Baker's chocolate
1 cup boiling water
2 cups sugar
½ cup butter or margarine
½ teaspoon salt
2 eggs, separated
1 cup buttermilk
1 teaspoon soda
1 teaspoon vanilla
2½ cups cake flour

Melt the chocolate and add the boiling water, boiling until thick. Cool. Cream sugar and butter, add salt and egg yolks. Into the buttermilk put soda and vanilla. Add alternately with cake flour. Fold in stiffly beaten egg whites. Bake at 350° in two 8″ layer pans, 30 minutes.

A fudge frosting is good on this cake, or a fluffy white frosting, because it is a moist, tender cake.

Easy Chocolate Cake

2 cups sugar
2 cups flour
1 cup margarine
¼ cup cocoa
1 cup water
½ cup buttermilk
1 teaspoon soda
1 teaspoon vanilla
2 eggs

Sift sugar and flour. Combine margarine, cocoa, and water in a saucepan and bring to a boil. Pour over sugar and flour mixture. Blend. Add buttermilk, eggs, soda, and vanilla. Mix well. Pour into greased 10" x 15" pan. Bake at 400° for 20 minutes. Prepare icing 5 minutes before cake is done. Spread on cake immediately after it is out of the oven.

Icing for Easy Chocolate Cake

½ cup margarine
¼ cup cocoa
6 tablespoons milk
1 box powdered sugar
1 teaspoon vanilla

Nancy Johnson cooked supper for our Paul to prove she was a good cook, and when Paul came home he brought me a sample of her cake. He was so proud of it! It is good.

War Cake

2 cups sugar
1 cup lard
1 pound raisins
¼ teaspoon salt
2 cups water
4 cups flour
2 teaspoons cinnamon
2 teaspoons cloves
1 heaping teaspoon of soda
  dissolved in hot water

Boil the first 5 ingredients 5 minutes and cool. Sift dry ingredients together. Add to the wet mixture along with the dissolved soda. Bake at 350° for 40 minutes. This one is an old favorite from Nora Litwiller's recipe collection.

Low-Calorie Carrot Cake

1 cup flour
½ cup granulated sugar
  or 1 tablespoon sweetener
⅓ cup sugar
2 teaspoons baking powder
1 teaspoon cinnamon
½ teaspoon soda
½ teaspoon vanilla
¼ teaspoon salt
1 cup shredded carrots
2 eggs
½ cup oil
¼ cup chopped nuts
¼ cup raisins

Blend all the ingredients and beat for 3 minutes. At the last fold in ¼ cup chopped nuts and ¼ cup raisins. Bake in 8″ square pan, greased and floured, for 35 to 40 minutes at 350°. A toothpick inserted comes out clean when it's done. Sprinkle with powdered sugar. This makes 16 servings of 160 calories each. It is a cake that borderline diabetics can eat. Doris Lock makes it for people who need special dishes.

$250 Red Cake

½ cup shortening
1½ cups sugar
2 whole eggs
2 ounces red food coloring
1 teaspoon vanilla
2½ cups flour
1 teaspoon salt
2 tablespoons cocoa
1 cup buttermilk
1 tablespoon vinegar
   and 1 teaspoon soda

Cream shortening and sugar, add eggs and food coloring which may be 1 ounce coloring plus 1 ounce water. Sift together dry ingredients and add alternately with the buttermilk. Beat after each addition at medium mixer speed. Add vanilla, vinegar and soda mixed together, mix well. Bake 40 minutes at 350° in two large layer pans. This will be a generous cake.

Cooked Topping for Red Cake

1 cup milk
¼ cup flour
1 cup sugar
1 cup margarine
   or shortening

Cook milk and flour; cool. Beat sugar and shortening at high speed until fluffy. Combine with cooked mixture and add 1 teaspoon vanilla. Beat well. Julie bakes this cake for David's birthday and other special occasions.

Pound Cake

2¼ cups flour
1 box powdered sugar
5 eggs, separated
1 whole egg
1 teaspoon vanilla
½ cup milk
½ pound butter
1 teaspoon nutmeg

Cream butter. Add sugar gradually. Add 5 egg yolks, one at a time, and mix. Add whole egg and mix. Sift flour and nutmeg and add to mixture, alternately with milk. Beat egg whites until stiff and fold into mixture. Bake in ungreased, floured tube pan at 350° for 1 hour. Rebecca likes old-fashioned recipes so she uses this one.

Ruby Rhubarb Cake

4 cups chopped rhubarb
6 ounces red gelatine
1½ cups water
yellow cake mix

Rub the baking dish with butter or margarine. Spread rhubarb pieces over bottom and sprinkle with the dry red gelatine and sugar. I like to use strawberry-flavored gelatine. I also use more rhubarb, as much as 6 cups, because I like a fruity dessert. Mix yellow cake according to package directions and pour over the chopped rhubarb mixture. Bake according to cake directions. This will make a thick 9″ x 13″ cake. If you prefer more fruit and less cake, put it in a larger pan. It goes down well with the men around my table at corn-planting time.

An old favorite Mother used to have on hand when Dad and I came home from school around George Washington's birthday was Cherry Cake.

Cherry Cake

½ cup butter or margarine
1½ cups sugar
2 eggs
1 cup sour milk
1 cup drained cherries (canned)
1 teaspoon soda
1 teaspoon cinnamon
2 cups flour
½ cup chopped hickory nuts

Mother would put the cherries she had canned last summer into a sieve to drain while she mixed the shortening, sugar, and eggs. She sifted together the dry ingredients and used cherry juice to sour the milk. She baked it in two 8″ round cake tins well greased and floured for 30 minutes. When it was cooled, she topped it with caramel icing.

Jonathan has always begged me to make Cowboy Coffee Cake for snacks for hay makers at 3 p.m., served with glasses of iced tea. It may have come originally from a chuckwagon cook out on the range who threw together cake for the cowboys. It goes down equally well with modern-day cowboys. Of course, on hot days out west milk was always sour.

Cowboy Coffee Cake

2½ cups flour
½ teaspoon salt
2 cups brown sugar
⅔ cup shortening
2 teaspoons baking powder
½ teaspoon soda
½ teaspoon cinnamon
½ teaspoon nutmeg
1 cup sour milk
2 well-beaten eggs

Combine flour, salt, sugar, and shortening; mix until crumbly. Reserve ½ cup to sprinkle over batter. To the remaining crumbs, add baking powder, soda, and spices; mix thoroughly. Add milk and eggs; mix well. Pour into 2 waxed-paper-lined 8″ pans; sprinkle with reserved crumbs. Chopped nutmeats and cinnamon may also be sprinkled over crumbs. Bake in moderately hot oven 25 minutes. I also use a 9″ x 13″ pan, which can be greased and floured well, to avoid use of paper.

Quick Coffee Cake

Mix prepared yellow cake mix and pour into greased and floured pan of appropriate size. Sprinkle on any combination of these ingredients: chopped nuts, brown sugar, butter pieces, coconut, or maple syrup. Bake 25 minutes at 350°. Rebecca fixes this quick cake to take to the field to the men. She also does it for Sunday night snacks. Farmer's wives need to know the shortcuts.

When Johnny Appleseed sat at meat with Squire Jesse Adams in his home in New Hampshire, there was much good visiting about the travelers who worked their way into the "wild west" of Ohio and Indiana. Johnny himself traveled a lot, spreading his apple seeds as he went, hoping to see apple orchards spring up to feed the westward bound pioneers.

When Ella Boyles moved into Lacon and came to our house to buy fresh country eggs we visited and I showed her our new baby, Rebecca. We saw them frequently and visited often. When she told me she was a Chapman, descended from Johnny Appleseed Chapman, and I found in my family tree that he had visited in my great, great-grandfather's home, our mutual admiration was heightened.

Mrs. Ella Boyles has been a family friend since Rebecca's birth in 1953. She has taken care of all of our children in addition to being my piano accompaniest when I sing. Eighty-eight years young, she is still a very pleasant traveling companion.

I was beginning to speak at various women's meetings and I liked to close my talk with a song. Ella is an accomplished pianist, having been a player in the old silent movie house when she was a girl. She and I collaborated on many songs and musical programs. We logged many miles of traveling together. She is a pleasant companion. We still travel together as she approaches her eighty-eighth birthday.

She has babysat all of our children. They loved to have her come and read storybooks to them. She remembers Maryanne begging her to tell about her own girlhood on the farm. Paul went to her house while I taught junior choir class on Friday afternoons. She would read to him till he fell asleep where I would find him after choir class.

Mrs. Boyles gave me this favorite recipe she makes for her son and for potluck suppers.

Wonder Buns

1 package or 1 large cake yeast
½ cup lukewarm water
½ teaspoon sugar
½ cup warm water
3 tablespoons sugar
3 tablespoons melted shortening
1 teaspoon salt
1 egg
3¼ cups flour

Stir yeast in water and sugar and let stand 10 minutes. Combine the other ½ cup warm water, sugar, melted shortening, and the salt in a large bowl and let stand 10 minutes also. Stir in dissolved yeast. Add the egg, stir well, then add flour. Knead until smooth. Make into buns right away. Let rise until double in size and bake at 400° for 15 minutes, or when brown enough.

Another friend of ours, Dorothy Kiefer, sent me this extra-tender and delicious recipe for rolls good enough for dessert.

Frosted Cinnamon Twists

¾ cup milk
⅓ cup sugar
1 teaspoon salt
½ cup shortening or margarine
2 cakes of yeast (or packages)
1 well-beaten egg
3¼ to 3⅓ cups enriched flour

Scald milk, pour over sugar, salt, and shortening in bowl. Stir and let stand until lukewarm. Crumble yeast in mixture. Stir until dissolved; put in egg, add flour, mix thoroughly with your hand. Turn out on floured board and knead until smooth and elastic. Place in greased bowl and cover with damp cloth. Let rise until doubled in bulk. Punch down and let rise again until almost doubled. Punch down. Roll dough on floured surface into oblong 6" x 24". Spread surface with 2 tablespoon soft butter or margarine and sprinkle with 3 tablespoons sugar and 1 teaspoon cinnamon. Cut in 1" strips and twist like a figure eight. Press ends so they don't unwind. Place on greased cookie sheet. Cover with damp cloth. Let rise until light. Bake 25 minutes at 375°. While slightly warm, top with confectioner's sugar icing. This can be made from 1 cup powdered sugar and 2 tablespoons milk.

One day when Ralph was grinding hog feed in the big bank barn, he came in and asked me if I would like some homeground cornmeal and cracked wheat. I was glad to get both. Then I started looking for recipes. I came upon this one that works well for us. It is full of roughage and good for what ails you.

Whole Wheat Bread

1 package dry yeast (dissolve in ¼
    cup lukewarm water and let rise)
1 tablespoon brown sugar
Scald 1¾ cups milk (or ¾ cup milk
    and 1 cup potato water)
Pour on 3 tablespoons melted lard
2 teaspoons salt
1½ tablespoons brown sugar
Cool to lukewarm, 80°

Add 3 cups of flour, then the yeast, then 3 cups more flour. It may take a little more depending on the kind of flour you use. I add some of my coarse ground wheat here. Heat oven 2 minutes for a warm place to raise dough.

Stir until you can't stir any more in. Turn on floured board. Knead 7 to 10 minutes, adding flour if necessary to keep from sticking. Put in greased crock. Grease top of dough lightly. Cover with towel. Place in 85° temperature. Let rise till doubled in size. (If your flour is too coarse it won't double in size.) Allow about 2 hours. Punch down, knead lightly, cut into 2 parts. Leave on board, let rise about 40 minutes. Punch down and shape into 2 loaves. Put in greased bread pans (tin is best). Let double about 45 minutes. Put in oven at 350° for 15 minutes. Set temperature back to 325° for 35 minutes more. It's a firm loaf, not high and light. Natural wheat germ breads, no matter how dark or firm, are preferred by many.

I am a health enthusiast and believe nature includes in her foods all the necessities for good nutrition; also plenty of laxative foods if we eat them. Whole grain cereals are the best. I have a custom of cooking wheat in wintertime. It is merely the wheat from the grain bin. Grain is washed, soaked on low heat to soften until it is tender enough to cook, and eaten in its plain goodness. For breakfast a small bowlful with sugar and cream is enough, both as to chewing exercise and nutritional value.

Several years ago we spread our arms and embraced a whole beautiful family, welcomed into our midst a young couple with a two-week-old baby, and rejoiced that all our family could return to be with us again.

We set the dining room table with fifteen plates. A young man looking for a family came to eat, newlyweds shared our board, and of course our twenty-nine-year-old Polish farm trainee, who still wonders at our way of living, was here.

Tame rabbit, chicken, pork, beef roasts, and whole wheat bread passed under our hands and became food for the hungry multitude when the mercury dipped to fifteen below zero two mornings, consecutively. Scores of pancakes were flipped off our griddle for breakfast, and pints of maple syrup from our own trees were poured on them to sweeten an already happy occasion.

Jonathan, age ten, was disturbed about being left out of the bowling party until he was enlisted to make a cake for Sunday dinner. We decorated it with "Praise God 1977." In asking the diners what they each had to praise God about, it came out that Tim and Sandy were going to have a baby in July! Then the festivities increased, and the whole table was rollicking with laughter and good will.

For Saturday afternoon sport the younger set took shovels and carved a huge snow house with three tunnels leading to the main room in the center of an eight-foot drift in our back ditch. It was exciting and fun to crawl into. We all had to try it. The extreme cold had made the snow hard, just the way Eskimos like it.

Here in the middle of the winter we heard our son David speak to our congregation Sunday morning at church with the message that God loved us enough to send his Son Jesus Christ, to be the bridge, the Savior, the answer to our perplexed lives.

Paul's chamber choir sang at the church youth service and he led the scripture reading and prayer. When he came home he found triplet lambs born to one ewe, so he remained very busy through the weekend. Ralph helped Julie's dad, Don, get a tractor scoop loaded to take home. The men visited from the time they met till they parted. Rebecca and Dale came in Sunday for the service and stayed to spend the afternoon. Rebecca did chores with me.

I snatch these precious moments with my grown-up children and treasure them. I hope they like them as well. I know how my mother feels when I call her on the phone to talk, or when we are together to visit and share things we have been thinking and meditating on. Life is so short. The change of generations is upon us.

I don't mind sweeping the rugs, folding up the chairs, putting away the table leaves, putting away extra bedding and doing the laundry. I'm grateful all this happened here in our home and did not pass us by. The cardinal outside my window picking at the birdseed seems to agree. It's nice to be around people who give and love and live.

Intermission

The Family of
"The Farmer's Wife"

One

Who am I? Where did I come from? These questions are in every child's vocabulary.

Each has the right to know his background, her heritage. More than that, each of us needs to know why we are living now. Who knows but that we have been "called" for such a time as this?

In the search for identity we go from our forebears to the now. We search our reason for being, and we look to the future. Where are we going? What is our reason for living?

Somewhere along the line the child of God emerges and asks to inherit the kingdom of heaven. All this and heaven, too, is our great gift . . . and our destiny.

My four grandparents had ancestry from the European continent and England. Those who contributed to my heredity were each different indeed. I try to imagine the romance of the past, realizing that I did not even know two of them, Father's parents, except to hear about them. Fortunately, a family passes on stories that help you to sketch the lives of important people you just missed knowing, but wish you had.

In northeastern Indiana, not too far from Fort Anthony Wayne of French and Indian War fame, lived four young people in the early 1800s who were destined to be my grandparents.

About 1880 the sixteen-year-old Julia Ann Barfell met a dashing young Frenchman, Eugene Bobilya. He was a farmer who hauled logs during the winter months to the stave factory at New Haven. The two had grown up about four miles apart in Allen County and became acquainted. In due time they married and in 1892 came to live on the farm at the corner of the Barkley and Clayton roads which has been the Bobilya homestead ever since.

They had identical twin boys, and three more before a girl came to round out their family. They were sturdy, strict parents, bringing Julia Ann's English-German traditions and Eugene's French Huguenot ancestry to their children. The August Bobilier who immigrated from Europe was an itinerant painter, but little more is known, partly because of Americanizing the family name from Bobilier to Bobilya. I've often yearned to search that branch of my roots but have had little help.

My father, Clarence Lucius, was born the fourth child on August 28, 1887. He told us little of his early childhood. Perhaps he was sad about it. He tells about how the family used to go to his grandparent's home for Christmas with horses pulling the sleigh. The older brothers hunted cross-country all the way while he had to carry the burlap bag of rabbits they shot. The rabbits were skinned and hung across the clothesline to freeze before they proceeded with Christmas celebrating and dinner.

The hardwoods stood so thick in those days that Grandpa Bobilya could stand at his back door and shoot squirrels for food. The boys acquired the skill of hunting early. My father brought home game occasionally for my mother to cook although he always expressed sorrow over having to kill.

Grandma Bobilya tried to rear her boys right and didn't approve of some of the skills they brought home. She threw their playing cards into the cookstove. Dad was a younger and more sensitive son whom her wrath did not often touch.

Grandpa Bobilya raised fine horses. Horse breeders who used foul language came to their farm. Again Grandma didn't approve. She was a good mother. A dark shadow

103

came across their home when she died of cancer at age forty-six. My father missed his high school graduation for her funeral, but he had acquired enough of her Puritan precepts to form the morals that guided his life. It is a fitting tribute to Grandma and Grandpa that on the morn of her death Grandpa Bobilya opened the Bible to read aloud as was his custom. He read the entire eighth chapter of Romans to the grieving family, including, "All things work together for good to them that love God, to them who are the called according to his purpose."

My father began his first year of public school teaching in 1908. He was an active churchman and taught Sunday school classes. He and his brothers were baseball playing friends of Lloyd Douglas, their minister's son. After Dad knew him, the Rev. Mr. Lloyd Douglas proceeded to carve out a name for himself as author of several best sellers in the 1940s, among which are the novels, *The Robe, The Big Fisherman* and *Magnificent Obsession.* My father took me to visit him shortly before he died. The great author is indelibly impressed on my memory.

Dad lived with his bachelor brother, Amos, on the home farm and taught the eight grades of common school in Madison Township for several years. World War I was looming on the horizon, so he sang the old songs and recited patriotic poetry to his pupils. How often I've heard the story of how he almost was conscripted into the service just before the armistice was signed on the eleventh hour of the eleventh day of the eleventh month of 1918.

One fine day at Allen County Teacher's Institute in Fort Wayne he spied a winsome dark-haired French girl. She was Inez Edna Bandelier, the young schoolmistress of Whitney School in Jefferson Township. She admired the tall, lean, handsome, dark-haired man who gave fiery oratorical readings. He proceeded to win her heart.

My father and mother, Clarence and Inez Bobilya of Monroeville, Indiana, are shown here in a photograph taken shortly before their golden wedding anniversary. They were the "twig benders" in my life who made my childhood years so happy.

My mother's ancestry is more familiar to me because I knew both Grandma and Grandpa Bandelier for many of their later years. Mother has told me about her grandmother who was a Yankee from Maine. That young girl remembered Indians pushing into their cabin and roasting a turtle in the fireplace during an overnight "visit."

The Adamses of the Revolutionary War period and relatives of presidents John and John Quincy Adams had children who came west from New Hampshire. Among the descendants of squire Jesse Adams, justice of the peace for Jefferson Township, Indiana, was Mary Adelaide. She married the young Frenchman, Emmett Bandelier, from the Canton of Berne in Switzerland when she was nineteen years old.

I thrilled whenever Grandpa Bandelier told me the story of his coming to this country as a boy on a small sailing vessel with his two brothers to join their father in America after their mother died. I could see them singing their French songs to pay their passage. They then worked their way west to Allen County.

Emmett, a sandy haired, small-built man, farmed with his father. He became proficient with machinery and ran a steam engine for threshing grain. He bought his own farm before he married Mary Adelaide in 1889. They had three boys and three girls, among whom was Inez, the eldest daughter, born in 1894. Her nickname was "Smiles."

Grandpa and Grandma Bandelier made a happy home. He was mechanically inclined and worked on several inventions related to hydraulics which he did not patent. I loved to watch Grandpa work at his tool bench or hoe in the garden. They lived on sandy soil and had large berry patches. Mother tells of picking strawberries her mother would serve sweetened to eat on fresh baked bread. Grandma sewed for her grandchildren, read us stories and was plump and loving. She died of pneumonia when she was seventy-four years old. Grandpa lived many years longer, till he was a venerable ninety-six.

My dad came to visit Mother in his Model T Ford and enjoyed courting her in the big, happy family environment. He was lonely for family life and enjoyed even the youngsters who perched on the stairway out of sight the night he proposed to Mother. "Those pesky kids," Mother would say. My uncles and aunts would chuckle about it.

Dad wrote passionate poetry about her and published three songs, "Come Now Theresa, Won't You Biplane with Me?"; "Cuddle Close Beside Me Rob and Call Me 'Love' for It's Leap Year you Know"; and "Hurrah for Woody Wilson." The little Model T Ford figured in an accident they had with an interurban train where she was almost killed. They were married in a beautiful wedding ceremony on May 15, 1918.

My parents bought and farmed the home place. While they were newlyweds one summer, they built a tent in the front yard and slept out under the oak trees in Wah Tung. I enjoy telling our children this story because they have a hard time believing grandparents were ever young and romantic. Mom and Dad were popular with the young people in the neighborhood, too. Aunt Esther came to live one school year with them before I was born. Dad's nephew, Eugene, also came to live with us after I was born.

Along with feeding hired men, Mother ran a busy household. She worked especially hard when I was three. That year we moved into a nearby schoolhouse to allow a new, two-story bungalow to be built over the old house frame. Those days are the first I remember.

In a photograph taken a few years ago, my mother, "Grammie," holds Jennifer Lynn Wier, her great-grandchild. Mother recently celebrated her eighty-sixth birthday and still resides on the Indiana home farm. She takes an active interest in her family and neighbors and greatly enjoys ours visits.

I grew up surrounded by love. Daddy and Mother took me to Massillon Church. I remember the Christmas program when I sang a little song, "When My Momma's Busy," rocking in my chair with my doll, Anna Mae. I had to be awakened to sing it, and I promptly fell asleep again when I was done. Not long afterward the old country church was closed and we went to St. Mark's Church in Monroeville. I still call that my home church in Indiana, the one in which Ralph and I were married.

Mother and I had many happy days together while Daddy taught school. I remember best the way Mother sang the old hymns. She still does. I begged her to play the piano for me and she always found time to do it. We had noon livestock chores to do. We would gather eggs, feed chickens, pluck geese, garden, and do all the seasonal things such as going to the woods and bringing back spring flowers or a pocketful of hickory nuts.

In the winter Mother ground the popped corn left over from the gathering around the cookstove the night before when neighbors Paul Schamerloh or Bill Barfell came to exchange the news. Mother taught me how to eat ground popcorn with fresh milk and sugar in a bowl. To this day I like that flavor, although my family laughs at me.

Then it was the fall of 1928 and I was going to be five years old. Daddy went off to school again, leaving me behind with a necktie draped around my shoulders, wishing I could go along. I begged for "Tanny, Bookie and Green Circle" which meant he was to stop at Boston, a store between us and the schoolhouse, and bring home candy and Beechnut Chewing Gum with a green circle on its wrapper. If he could or couldn't buy those for me, I still wanted him to bring me a book to look at. I wanted so badly to learn to read.

Elaine Hoffman gave me her **First Reader** one day when I was permitted to visit Daddy's school. That did it. I started to school, even though I am told that one day I had an accident and the teacher had to bring me home for dry bloomers!

There were three or four in my first grade and I loved it. I am so glad I went to Dad's one room school that year I turned five. There were Christmas exercises and a George Washington cherry tree with crepe paper cherries in February. The older boys and girls of the eight grades enacted a real play, **Mrs. Wiggs of the Cabbage Patch.** The next year schools all over the township were consolidated into one big school in Hoagland. Father and I went there together in a green Plymouth.

I was in Miss Marquardt's room which had grades one and two. I liked it, although I do remember paddlings some children got in front of the whole classroom. We had a beautiful music teacher, Miss Bailey, and an art teacher, Miss Thomas, who opened up the wonderful world of the arts to me. I was hooked on school from the beginning.

The big depression of 1929 didn't touch me, although my parents felt many repercussions. Money was hard to come by for paying off the mortgage on the farm. I remember a favorite dress of mine was made out of Daddy's old suit. Mother was clever with a needle and made all of my clothing. She pedaled her sewing machine early and late. Doll clothes, aprons, dustcaps, dish towels, underwear, curtains, sheets, and gifts for all came from her magic machine.

I read nursery rhymes from memory because Mother had taught them to me. We sang them to little tunes. I taught my dolls the same ones. Then came fairy tales. I had to read them all, but I didn't like the gory ones. I didn't even care for the three trolls that lived under the bridge.

My early years were happy on our farm with neat square fields. When I wasn't lying in the grass out under the lilac bush playing with the dog, I was "helping" Mom and Dad. Farm animals have been part of my life. There was always a bucket calf to raise, maybe three. I remember Fudge and Taffy who earned their names because one led easily and the other was hard to pull. I had rabbits for a short time, but cats and a dog were always beside me. My pony, Billy, was trained to pull a cart. It was popular to hitch him up and have him haul the cousins around on Sunday afternoons, if we could make him go. Quite often he balked and stopped right in the middle of the front yard near where the adults were visiting, seated on chairs under the spreading red oak trees, as if he were begging for them to release him from those bothersome kids.

The milk cows were really pets. All were named and had individual personalities, even to knowing which one would tear her yoke off trying to go through the fence. Before I learned to milk the cows, my parents relegated me to playing a safe distance away. I pretended to make cheese in the big stock tank because I knew how to make cheese! Our milk went to a cheese factory and I had been through it. Or I would sit on the rusty iron seat of the old hay rake thinking I was driving a team of horses, working the levers, dumping hay at intervals.

Soon I was old enough to go barefooted across the pasture to get the cows in the evening. Then, morning and evening, it became my chore. The dog accompanied me. I begged hard for a pony to ride after the cows, and that is why Billy was lent to us for a few seasons. I rode him until I was so big my feet touched the ground.

I didn't milk cows until I was older because it was serious business to get all the milk Mother and Dad could skillfully pull out of each teat. The milk check was a regular part of our small income and very important. When the day came to learn the grip of milking, I was told not to dig in my nails but to squeeze and pull down gently. My desire was to make the milk foam up in the bucket like Dad and Mom, but it was awhile before my hands were strong enough.

I started on old Faunie. Then Goldie, with the big udder, who was an easy milker. I was permitted to milk her all the way, stripping out the last drops. Those warm summer evenings when we three sat in the barnyard near the water tank and milked were times of visiting and enjoying the cooling night air after a hard day's work.

Summertime was green apple time when I could lie along the big lower limb of the sweet apple tree and munch its fruit. Dad made for me a rubber tire swing. I mostly played alone because no neighbors had children my age. Often I was with my father. I remember the time I caught my leg in a moving part of the grain drill. He carried me to the house. I still have that scar on my ankle. That didn't keep me away from farming, however. I rode Old Whitey every time I could coax her to the gate and hop on. Once I flew over her head when she was galloping. She stepped over me instead of on me. The air was knocked out of me, but I was unhurt. I felt proud whenever the accident was retold. The same thing reocurred later when I was riding too close to the back of the hay wagon and the team started up, spilling me over backward.

In the haze of my childhood, every new day started with a rosy sunrise and ended with the whole western sky aglow behind our big green hip-roofed barn. I cannot even remember a rainy day because Mother made such pleasant weather inside the house. I was secure in my parents' love. The world was very far away except when some special person came to Fort Wayne, eighteen miles from our house.

The most cherished people were Grandma and Grandpa Bandelier, Lloyd Douglas, my music teachers (especially the violin teacher who had skiied over the Alps in World War I with a machine gun on his back), and Charlie Brouwer. Charlie was the corner groceryman one mile from our farm. He ran a huckster wagon past our place weekly with groceries, kerosene, notions, even yard goods. I watched for him long before he came into view because it was a big event to go out and shop with Mother. I might get a stick of striped candy.

Looking back on it now, I believe these visitors were among the most important people in the world. They influenced many other little boys and girls like myself and formed in our minds the morals that would guide us in the future.

Many days I played alone, making pretty mudpies or catching crawdads in the creek. I made my own mechanical invention from an old sewing machine frame and played "threshing machine" with it. I hauled things on my green wooden wagon and played with the dog and cats, taking them for rides or carrying kittens in a basket to the neighbors' houses.

I kept away from the buck sheep after a skirmish with him when Mother had to fight him to rescue me. Even the hired man jumped and broke through the floor of our old buggy trying to get away from him.

I was a hardy country girl. There were no clouds on my horizon when winter approached. I loved the snow, sliding, and skating. When it was snowing I felt secure indoors with my dolls, books, and puzzles. I remember staying close to the oven door, which was open a lot of the time for more heat. We had no fireplace in our "modern" house, so we sat in the kitchen around the big, black, silver-trimmed cookstove.

It seemed that Daddy always had school papers to grade, but there was always time for Bible reading ending with the Lord's Prayer. Then we all went up the stairs to the cold bedrooms till morning.

Holidays were played to the hilt. At Easter my pile of clothes in the bathroom held a nest of colored eggs. At Christmas my shoes had oranges in them. We always celebrated every special day with a treat to eat. Our mainstay at ordinary suppertimes was fried potatoes and eggs, but we could count on a cake or pie for dessert on special days.

Mother canned all kinds of good food. We had fruit in winter when most people went without. We had green vegetables, too, because every summer there was a big garden beside the orchard.

I learned to work in the garden against my will, just to hear Dad and Mother tell stories. I have entranced our own children working in our garden with some of the same stories. Dad always had a proverb, maxim, or saying to fit each occasion. In fact, he had a whole book of them in his head. I liked to hear my parents quote poetry, taking turns, verse after verse. I lived with knowledge and therefore spent most of my evenings studying or living inside storybook pages with princes, fairies, animals, and elves.

Very early I learned birds by name, then recognized trees in our woods. We picked wildflowers every spring. When Dad took me with him when he built fence, the success of the day lay in how many bird's nests we found in the corners of the rail fence. When woven wire fence was to be put up, we always moved nests carefully if we couldn't leave them untouched.

Dad was a farmer, besides being a teacher. Summertime brought long hours in the fields. I learned to drive a team of horses after I proved myself on old Whitey. At first I rode her home after meeting father a long way up the road when he came home from the east forty. For safety I held onto the hames. The salty sweat of the horse's back stung my legs, but that was heaven. The neighbors called me a tomboy.

Threshing days were wonderful. Jess Franz would bring the rig the night before and I would watch with Daddy when the steam engine was getting set for the next day's work of threshing oats or wheat. The biggest thrill of all was after everything was set and evening was closing in fast. He would let me climb up into the cab and pull the string on the steam whistle for one last "toot."

Threshing days usually dawned clear and bright. There wouldn't be threshing if it weren't that way. It was usually hot, and maybe humid, before the day was over. I had to watch from the front yard. Skittish teams pulled up beside whirling belts and sweaty men tossed bundles into the giant mouth of the separator. I heard the good-natured ribbings they gave each other.

I hung around the kitchen where three or four women cooked for a half day getting ready to feed the men at noon. I remember putting on my best cotton calico with an apron over it like Mother's. There was even a handkerchief in my apron pocket. If I were permitted to throw out the potato peelings to the chickens, gather the eggs, or put the dishtowels on the clothesline I was thrilled.

It soon became my job to get the soap, washpan, hand towels, and a comb outdoors by the back door for the men to clean up before they came in to eat. We women always waited on the men and ate at the second table with boys who might not have found a place at the men's table.

This whole process repeated itself at each of the neighbors' homes until the circle was finished, the threshing ring done. It was the biggest social event of late summer, and lasted the longest. Patterns and recipes were exchanged. Everybody got to see the inside of everybody's house. Mother was in high demand to make her butterscotch pie which I have included in this book.

Butchering day, corn shredding day, woodsawing day, and apple-butter-making day all brought the same thrill: big meals, Mother's butterscotch pie, and neighbors coming to help.

Two

There were many wonderful days for a child on the farm during the 1930s even though the depression worried most people. I was oblivious of it and knew only that it was a treat to have oranges, a new dress, or a trip to the circus in July when Daddy felt we could take a half day off from farming. Often we couldn't afford to go into the big top, but it was thrill enough to see the big parade on the downtown streets before the show began. Just to see the exotic circus girls, elephants, and striped tents was a rare treat; however, Dad was good at getting complimentary tickets from places where the big ads were plastered up. Whether or not we got inside the tent to see his favorites (lions and tigers) perform, he always bought a bag of California humpbacked peanuts to eat with it all.

I wasn't always cooperative. I remember one day Mother became quite irritated with my not wanting to work. All I wanted to do was read the book I was deep into, so she had me carry out a rocking chair and sit under the ripe cherry trees to keep away the birds. I doubt that I did a good job of that either.

In the field my diligence was better. I learned to drive with pride a team of horses hitched to the various farm implements. I helped Dad make hay and was glad that he trusted me to drive for him. He piled the hay on the hay wagon from the hayloader that poured the loose, dry livestock feed in swirls onto the rack. Then at the barn I learned to drive the team to pull the hayfork up into the mow. That was a big day when I was strong enough to lift the doubletrees with one hand and handle the team lines with the other. I could then do the job Mother had always done.

Hired men spiced up life for a country-born child. First and longest we had Morris Rose. He played the mouth harp at night after supper. He was a jolly man and a good worker, but the time Daddy paid him with a roll of one dollar bills was too much for him to take. He left to spend it and never came back. We had various boys Dad had taught in school. They were fun to have at the dinner table, but none stayed overnight. Daddy enjoyed baseball so much that after dinner when most men rested and read the newspaper the three of us would go out and bat around the ball.

Now, I realize Mother was in poor health after I was born and during my early childhood. But we had good times together, learning to color pictures, sew, cook, clean house, can vegetables and fruits, even meats. A series of operations cleared up her malady. She is enjoying the best of health in her later years.

If I had a picture to color, paper dolls to cut out or some craft to make, I could concentrate on it for hours. I saw that every flower, leaf, tree, or cloud in the sky had a symmetry of its own that I wanted to reproduce on paper. I grew to love my art classes in school. Music was another favorite. I started piano lessons early because Mother played the piano and sang. I wanted to do so too. She would play "Beautiful Ohio" for me whenever I lay sick; maybe even "Woodland Echoes."

Then came years of violin lessons. By the time I was in high school I was sure I wanted to be a singer. I heard grand programs on the old Zenith radio and tried to copy them.

In my teens I was star struck, too, and begged my tired parents to take me to a movie in Decatur once in awhile. It was too much expense to see one every week, but maybe once a month. Daddy might fall asleep, but Clark Gable, Jeannette MacDonald, Nelson Eddy, and Joan Crawford were greats in my collection of movie stars.

Each summer just before school began Dad would come down with hay fever. It was a real for sure attack of sneezing, runny nose, and weepy eyes. As often as we could we went north to get away from the ragweed that caused his sneezing. Vicksburg, Michigan, where Uncle Frank and Aunt Nora lived, was one stop, but farther up near the Straits was where we usually headed. This was at a time farm people seldom traveled. Sometimes Dad would drive us into Canada. It felt like going into a foreign country after customs officers inspected our suitcases! We usually turned around and came back shortly or exited on the other side of one of the Great Lakes.

Once we took Grandpa and Grandma Bandelier and made a grand tour of the eastern states, stopping at Washington, D.C., for almost a week. For the most part I only wanted to find a lake to wade in and, wonder of wonders, I finally owned a bathing suit. In 1934 we went to the Chicago World's Fair and in 1942 to the New York World's Fair. I walked in front of a camera and my parents in another tent could see me. It was the first television.

For many years I had the job of taking the cows a half mile on the road to pasture in the field on the east forty. This happened every morning and again in the evenings. I talked my parents into a bicycle for the job. That contrivance caused scarred knees, but I grew adept at managing it even in loose crushed rock.

My big desire, now, was a riding horse. I could handle the work horses. They were my special friends. We had a matched team of sorrels, Prince and Don. They were Dad's pride, but almost his undoing, too. Don was a runaway, and he scared all of us until Dad traded him. He was sorry to trade Don because Prince and Don had made a pretty match. We got Frank then, a clumsy Clydesdale, but we learned to love him, too. He was funny, but never funnier than the day he fell over sideways into the horse tank, feet up, while drinking with his harness on. We had to have our neighbor, John Hawkins with his new tractor, come and tip the tank over to dump him on his feet.

117

Mother and Dad practiced their Christian faith to the best of their ability, strict in prayers, church attendance and Bible reading. I went to catechism classes for two years before I became a church member. It was a big day when I committed as much of myself to the Lord as I understood how to do. We remembered the event with a family dinner and gifts on that Pentecost Sunday.

Mother and Dad lived their faith. He put on the back of our big green barn, "Get Right With God," and he meant it. It was the way of life for my parents. They took many jibes for that barn motto. All the world could see it. Apparently my parents had influence on their neighbors because they were and still are respected and loved.

Because of Mother's injury when I was born, I was an only child. I prayed for brothers or sisters but none came. My cousins' summer visits were highlights. Mary Lou and Helen Jeannette were city cousins with whom we had a peck of fun, from podding peas for canning while Daddy told stories to keep us at it, to sleeping out under the trees in the front yard with a binder canvas tent to keep off the dampness. We got scared, giggled, bitten by bugs and mosquitoes, but never quite forgot those times. Helen petted our beautiful milk cow, Daisy Mae, and liked her so well that we took a picture of her with her arm around the cow's neck.

In school I made good grades because I worked hard at it. The schoolteacher's daughter had to be a good student. I wanted to learn. When I went to the county spelling contest I was scared and misspelled "vegetable." It was a disgrace, but I worked at spelling until, with the help of Latin, I could sound out and spell well. I also enjoyed literature, biology, and writing classes.

I was shaping up at about age twelve and wanted to sew clothes for myself. I had already embroidered samplers and crocheted a little. Mother taught me most of what I knew about sewing. For a few years I belonged to 4-H club, the requirements of which were the best discipline. I've sewed clothing for myself all my life. It is good to know how to clothe yourself and your family. All girls should learn to sew.

When graduation came around I was the class valedictorian. We had only eighteen graduates. It was a rural school at the edge of Hoagland. Physical education had been a favorite and we dressed in blue, one-piece gymsuits. Basketball was a mania but girls' competition had just been done away with because of female disorders many good players seemed to suffer. That didn't stop me from playing hard in intramural games and turning my knee out of joint on occasion.

Dad coached a girls' softball team for several years. I even came home from college weekends to play. We had a group of heavy hitters and won most of the time.

I grew up with farm animals and nature. Little wonder my parents were apprehensive when I started to college in a city. Living on campus was different from living at home on the farm, but finally Dad bought me my riding horse, Bonnie, and I enjoyed weekends when I could come home and ride her. I groomed her, cared for her, showed her in three-gaited classes in horse shows and was proud when she won ribbons!

Growing up is a gradual process. College was only the beginning of it for me. I enjoyed those halls of learning. I was free to date for the first time. The music and art departments saw most of my waking hours; however, I enjoyed physical education classes where I learned to swim, bowl, play tennis, and archery. I became active in the drama club and designed sets for productions. Knowing the professors was education at its best. Performers I'd read about came to our campus. There were parties and many good friends.

I barely felt ready for a position in society when I became a schoolteacher on graduation from Ball State Teacher's College in 1944. World War II was raging. Many college boys had gone to service.

I began teaching music and art in three grade schools in

Wayne Township near Fort Wayne. Living at home, I bought a little used Ford car, Betsy, and filled it with rationed gasoline to drive back and forth among the schools.

Three years passed. High school chorus and music appreciation classes were added to my schedule. I loved my pupils and had fun with them. Teaching was a challenge. Those were busy years, producing three grade school operettas and a high school musical each year.

I became ill with the most serious disease of my life when a feverish little first grader came to me in music class and asked me to take her home. She had scarlet fever. I contracted it and became very sick even though the new drug, sulfa, was used to treat it.

For a couple years I had been studying voice with a teacher in Fort Wayne who urged me to continue my studies in Chicago. There was much hesitancy among my people about my going to such an evil city. I was almost twenty-four and I still listened to my parents and their wishes. But I reasoned with them that I wanted to pursue my ambitions. In short, I had to see if the grass really was greener on the other side of the fence.

In September of that year, instead of my going back to teaching, my parents and I decided to go on a train tour of the rim of the west from Texas to the Canadian Rockies. We thoroughly enjoyed all of it. We made lifelong friends. The trip helped Dad out of the teaching routine of thirty-five years. He had retired from the schoolroom. Pullman trains and all, it was romantic making our way across the desert and through mountain passes. The diner was an experience in itself although the mashed potatoes tasted like fuel oil. We ate everything with gusto. The young people in our train spent a lot of time on the observation platform mainly because we thought it was so exciting to wave to people and see scenery without looking through a window. We made friends for life on that rollicking jaunt from Texas to the West Coast, up to Washington, and home through Lake Louise and Winnipeg.

In October I went to Chicago and found a job in a church office, got a room in a church girl's club, and reassured my parents that I was in good hands. I'm sure Mother's prayers followed me daily. I innocently trusted people and had a few close scrapes.

At work in the church offices in the Loop, they used me as staff artist, switchboard operator, and receptionist. Pastor E.W. Mueller, my boss, saw that I was a rural person through and through. He decided that I could well do a rural study of the duplication of Swedish, Norwegian, Finnish, Danish, German, and English ethnic churches in rural communities, some of which still preached the Word in their native tongue. I was more than ready to go after two winters of vocalizing, studying Italian for operatic work, and traveling the subway. Living in Chicago was a potpourri of good and bad things. There was the challenge of new work, new friends, and exciting surroundings. There were wonderful entertainment and educational opportunities if you could afford the time and money, but I had checked the greenness of the grass on the other side of the fence long enough.

I took an old car and my suitcase and traveled Wisconsin, Minnesota, South Dakota, North Dakota, Nebraska, and Iowa, talking with rural people about how their church served them. I asked them if it was time to put the ethnic backgrounds of the Lutheran church together into one healthy rural or town church. I learned to know a lot of wonderful people. Scandinavian pastries were often served by the

people I met.   Among the first and best recipes I collected is
this one.

Ranger Cookies

1 cup brown sugar

1 cup white sugar

1 cup shortening

2 eggs

1 teaspoon vanilla

1 teaspoon salt

1 teaspoon soda

1 teaspoon baking powder

2 cups flour

2 cups cornflakes (do not crush)

2 cups oatmeal

1 cup coconut

Mix shortening and sugar well, then add remaining
ingredients.   Drop by spoonfuls or roll and pat in shape with
palm of hand.   Bake at 325° for 12 minutes.

After the travels connected with the survey on church
duplication were over, I was asked to teach Bible school for
Pastor Norval Hegland in South Dakota.   I spent the most
enjoyable time of my life among the ranchers and Indians in
the sandhill country of northwest South Dakota.

Pastor Hegland was a flying preacher with a 400 square
mile parish.   He literally dropped me into isolated communities to stay with the people and teach their children the Bible. I
loved it, with kids eager to learn, and homes friendly to a
stranger amid the lonely wide open spaces.   It was out there
all alone I had my first real test and reassurance the Lord was
with me.

I had problems with the old car. One evening the water hose was leaking badly. It left me stranded miles from nowhere on a sticky gumbo road. The local ranchers had all gone home. I got out of my car to survey the situation. There were no telephone poles, no trees, no horses, nothing in sight but the fading western sunset. It was aglow with colors which reached halfway up the sky. I could have panicked, but I felt a quiet reassurance that the Lord was out here in this countryside, too. I calmed my thoughts of what might happen to me shivering alone all night in a stalled car. I saw melting snow in the ditch that might get my radiator filled again. With no bucket to dip it, I took off my shoe and carried it full back and forth until the engine was running safely and I got to a filling station for repairs.

After my job was finished I returned to Chicago only long enough to get ready to return home to teach another year of music and art in my home school. This was the third year Ralph and I had known each other from national rural youth meetings. I had been around the world a bit, been inspired by the fulltime Christian service in another rural part of the United States, and I had come to the realization that more than anything else, now I wanted to marry and have a family of my own.

While I worked in Chicago I studied with a Northwestern University teacher about the fine points of composition. I had a desire all my life to write. I wanted to describe my feelings and nature all around me. I had written several short articles, but I never had one published when I met Paul Johnson, editor of *Prairie Farmer* magazine. He was a friend of my boss, E.W. Mueller, and he took an interest in my article, "Why I Want to Marry a Farmer."

I wrote that it was the earnest desire of my life to have a farmer husband. My father had been a farmer and I admired him so much that I wanted to marry one, too. Mr. Johnson took issue with me on several points, edited the story severely, and printed it with a cover picture in June of 1950.

From it I received several proposals which all read the same, "I have so many head of hogs, so many head of cows, so many acres of land, I want you to meet my son . . . ."

I didn't answer any of them. I knew Ralph. I had been praying a year and a half for God's guidance in the matter of a husband. Ralph said I didn't mean what I had written, so I married him to prove it.

Three

The cemetery on top of Broaddus Hill just east of Lacon, Illinois, was unkempt and overrun with vines. Brush obscured all but the cement steps up to the site where the early settlers of the Wier family were buried. Then in 1976, during Bicentennial emphasis in our county to find and preserve the gravestones of ancestors, we arrived with saws and axes to clear the ground and give a semblance of respect to those of Ralph's family who had gone before. We erected an American flag at the grave of the original settler.

John and Catherine Wier came here from Virginia seeking a state sympathetic to the abolition of slavery. Their descendants have peopled this valley since 1832, farming these same lands, planting orchards, growing berries, crops of grain, and especially fine horses.

When I came here to live as a bride in 1951 the large red bank barn testified to the many fine horses that had been housed in its box stalls. I brought my contribution in the form of my American saddle horse, Bonnie, faithful companion of several years.

The homestead was old and lay in the valley below where the original cabin had set overlooking the Illinois River. The Wier family had a brickyard on this farm which provided the native red bricks for the house which was built next. That gave way to the large white frame structure we now live in. Ralph's parents brought him here in 1928 as a child, so he remembers it as the home he grew up in.

Ralph's father, Charles Eugene, was one of five children, and was born in 1892 to Fred and Anna Sperry Wier. Grandpa Fred Wier was a large man, upright, kind, handsome, gentle, and friend to all. His father had had an

125

inscription on his tombstone, "A friend to all," because he had reared twenty-one children, orphans, and hirelings who had come under his roof. Grandpa Wier died only a couple years before I came into the family. I regret never having met him because he had a great influence on Ralph.

On many occasions Ralph's grandfather influenced his thinking; they talked while walking in the timber under the spreading oaks. He told Ralph how he must continue the traditions brought down through the family. He also taught Ralph how to tap maple trees for syrup. Fred and Anna had worked hard and had many hired helpers to farm the land. The breeding of fine draft horses was one of Fred's passions. The Scotch-Irish heritage he carried well was embodied in his personality and integrity.

Anna Sperry was of English background, of a family of old settlers in the Lacon area. With such a large responsibility she had hired girls to help her clean, cook, and garden. She is remembered as helping to get the dinner on the large table at noon and then going to lie down and rest while the girls served it to the men. I became quite well acquainted with the tiny, friendly little lady before her death in 1960.

Grandpa and Grandma Wier moved into a large home across from the courthouse in town where Grandma ruled in fine style until Grandpa's passing, then continued as the family matriarch with faithful Alvina Zilm, her companion, caring for the house and cooking.

We brought our children to visit her each Sunday after church because her health kept her from worship services. She sat in her upholstered armchair in the living room where she could keep an eye on the comings and goings of all the townspeople. Nothing missed her keen eyes. She enjoyed holding each of our new babies as we presented them to her for approval. The other children rushed to the kitchen where

Sunday dinner would be cooking and Alvina passed out huge cream-colored sugar cookies. Here is the recipe:

Old-Fashioned Sugar Cookies

> ½ cup shortening
> 1 cup sugar
> 1 egg
> 3 cups flour (Alvina would
>   always knead a little
>   more flour into them.)
> ¼ teaspoon salt
> 3 teaspoons baking powder
> ½ cup milk
> ½ teaspoon vanilla extract

Cream shortening and sugar; add egg and beat well. Add sifted dry ingredients alternately with milk and vanilla; mix thoroughly. Chill dough before rolling. Lift with spatula to keep shape, after cutting. Sprinkle with sugar, if desired. Bake on greased cookie sheet at 350°, 10–12 minutes.

An era came to an end when Grandma Anna died. It was the passing of the time of the aristocrats and the dominions over which they ruled. Even the large white house with a tower, sleeping porch, and verandas on two sides went down under a wrecking ball because progress brought in a Texaco gas station. I didn't want to see that home go. It was a symbol to our children as well as subject for local artists.

Ralph's mother and father were practical, hard-working people who had grown up a mile apart as children. Emma Rickey was one of several children born to the union of Emma Smith and Charles Rickey. Her mother was of German background and was the short, plump, daughter of a farmer. In 1907 she died of dropsy when Ralph's mother, Emma Jane, her namesake, was eighteen years old. She left five girls and three boys to carry on the Rickey name.

Grandpa Rickey came from a large family in Pennsylvania to settle here and farm the bottomlands of the Illinois River valley. He was a tall, large man who enjoyed life, as verified in an old photograph of the Rickeys in an open touring car at a family reunion. But after his wife died he had a heart attack and was an invalid for many years. Ralph and his brothers and sisters remember him as he sat at the kitchen table playing solitaire late into the night. Perhaps he was lonely and

Charles and Emma Wier, Ralph's parents, lived close by. They posed for this photograph at the time of their forty-fifth wedding anniversary. After Mother Wier's death, Ralph's father came daily to supervise the farm work and to eat dinner with us at noon.

couldn't sleep. Murrie, Ralph's older sister, said he teased the grandkids and was good to them. He died of a stroke in 1931.

Charles Wier married Emma Rickey, the tall, dark-haired neighbor girl and schoolteacher, in 1916 and had three boys and two girls. The family grew up on this Wier homestead in the second bottoms of the Illinois River. Dad Wier took his wife and family to the LaRose Fair one summer day in a horse-drawn buggy. At the fair he unhitched the horse and raced her, winning third place. They were happy about the prize money, but the largest part of their lives was filled with work, dawn to dark.

Ralph was born in 1924 after an older brother, Wayne, and two sisters, Murrie and Lola Mae. A younger brother, John, followed him. Ralph grew up with machinery and remembers having to work horses in the field when he was but eight years old. When the time of the tractor came, he preferred it to horsepower. As with children today, the new, the modern and timesaving inventions spoke to him. I have told many people Ralph is a self-propelled, torque amplified, PTO kind of man. And that's a compliment in today's terms.

Ralph tells of a hard-working childhood, but there was fun, too. There were family dinners, fish fries, and homemade ice cream and watermelon feeds in the summertime. Christmas brought homemade candy. There always were dozens of cousins to ride horses, play ball and crack nuts. In the winter he made skiis from barrel staves to slide on the hills where our children ski today. He was a lover of nature, walking in the woods, listening to the birds. After his grandfather taught him to tap the maple trees he made syrup for the family for several years, taking pride in just the right flavor and color. Spiles were tapped into trees and buckets were hung. He and his brothers built a cooking shack in the grove and boiled down syrup many a night after they had gathered it with a team of horses and a sled. Work always seemed to be his play. His Grandfather Wier's talks with him inspired him to follow in his footsteps and be a pillar in the community when his turn came.

The family ran the Silver Maple Dairy for several years, delivering milk to customers in Lacon. Ralph and Wayne delivered the milk. Wayne met his future wife at a restaurant her father owned. Milking was a large item in the day's work. They still had a Holstein dairy farm of forty cattle when I came here to live. By that time there was a grade A milk truck picking up the cooled milk cans to take to Peoria for bottling. Gone were the days of little, local dairies selling unpasteurized milk.

Mother Wier was a beautiful soul who married a farmer and worked hard at the life she espoused. Her children learned lessons of perseverance at her side. She had a large vegetable garden and canned and preserved all her food. She was a charter member of the local home bureau, and when pressure canning was introduced by the extension service she picked up the process and was an early advocate of the method. Anything to better her family's life.

All farmsteads had chickens, but she raised fryers for sale besides the laying flock. Her daughters worked beside her dressing chickens for local patrons who came to buy. I followed the habit when we were first married and raised fryers for sale. But with five tiny children I soon stopped the business. However, Mother Wier came out early on the morning we dressed our fryers for our own freezer, and efficiently did two chickens to my one. We would have two tubs of chicken pieces cooling by noontime.

She damaged her health by overwork in the 1940s and had to have hired help in the house. It became evident that a heart condition had developed in the 1960s, but she was a faithful worker in her church. She loved her grandchildren and willingly came out to the farm to babysit when I needed to be away.

They had moved to a new home in town when we married and came to live on their farm. She baked goodies and brought them to the farm when she came out, and her plump body rocked all our babies to sleep. Her hobby was sewing.

She made clothes for her family and her grandchildren, and she was an ardent quilter at church. She was eager to be with her church friends, and for bazaars she worked on many aprons with her sister, Lena. Her heart condition worsened and she passed away in 1969.

She was a practical woman and I loved her. Always helpful, she supplied me with recipes when I needed them. One time, after bringing a butchered beef home to the freezer, I asked her for her recipe to use the raw suet in a suet pudding. She gave me this recipe.

Grandma Wier's Suet Pudding

> 1 cup ground suet
> 1 cup sorghum or brown sugar
> salt
> 2½ cups flour (or more for stiff batter)
> ½ teaspoon allspice
> ½ teaspoon nutmeg
> ¼ teaspoon cloves
> 1 teaspoon cinnamon
> 1 teaspoon soda
> 1 cup sweet or sour milk
> 1 cup raisins

Combine the ingredients as for a cake. Pour into greased coffee tins leaving plenty of space for rising. Cover or tie shut each container. Steam 1 to 1½ hours.

Dad Wier became more reclusive after Mother died, but he came to the farm regularly and farming was still his passion. He ate his noon meal with us at our table and did a man's work for several years. One day he fell and broke his hip while walking downhill. His working days were over. He was in the hospital and nursing home for a period of time and then came home to read books and be in his own house. He commented on how quickly a man can grow old. His shoulders stooped further and his walk was unsteady. Because of cataracts he drove nowhere but to the farm and finally that stopped. His loneliness engulfed him, and while his children came to minister to him, he was ready for another world. He died in 1976 and left the tradition of hard work for all who follow him. He had seen a depression. He had saved and been alert to opportunities when times got better. He bought land and was a successful farmer.

What effect did these four people, our children's grandparents, have upon our family? Only time will tell. The discipline and the pattern of two families set our course. Would it be too much to say that our children are the product of those people's ideals?

Four

Over in Illinois a young man was growing up, working, farming, praying, and he was intended for me. Soon the restlessness of days when we wondered why we had never met our future companion would be over. I never underestimate the unrest of the courtship years. They come on the heels of adolescence which alone can be painful. The temptations that present themselves at our most vulnerable time seem almost too large to surmount. In our case we turned to prayer for guidance.

Ralph was subject to draft during World War II but was rejected for a heart murmur. His feelings were crushed, but he worked quietly at home when being 4F was unpopular. The county agent interested him in rural youth activities of the Farm Bureau. It was through that organization he went to a national meeting of Rural Youth of the USA in 1947. I also was going to that meeting in Jackson's Mill, West Virginia, as a representative of the rural church office where I worked. I needed a ride and wrote the national secretary about it. She suggested that I contact Ralph Wier who was driving. He might be willing to pick me up enroute.

That day in October in Dwight, Illinois, was the first time I saw Ralph as I stepped off the bus to go with him to the national conference. He was friendly and kind, and I trusted him completely as we traveled to the university to meet a group of young people also going from Illinois. This was my element. I enjoyed the company of the rural youth and their clean-cut fun. In years to come, Ralph and I got to know each other very well through travel to and from national rural youth meetings.

Enroute home I stopped to show my parents this fine young man. They liked him. Then he took me back to my job in Chicago. We saw each other occasionally the next three years, but both of us dated other young people. It was not until a visit to Indiana in January of 1951 that he showed me the engagement ring he wanted me to have. He laughs about my being dazzled by it. The morning was frosty and the sun sparkled on every shrub and tree along the road. It was 8 a.m., and he was driving me to teach school when he made his proposal. I hesitated only long enough to realize that a bright new path of life was opening up before me in answer to my prayers for the last year and a half.

After I realized that I had found the man I was to marry (Ralph seemed to know sooner), we did not hesitate to set our wedding day. It was June 24, 1951, six months after we had become engaged. Oh, the lovely excitement of those months, the planning and designing of my wedding dress which I made. The finish of the schoolteaching year almost exhausted me with the presentation of a large musical. Mother and Dad held up well under all the work and festivities. We were married a month after my teaching job had ended. It was a beautiful church wedding, with a large circle of friends. The reception was held on that Sunday evening at my parents' home as the sun was setting, and well-wishers overflowed the big yard, front porch, and house.

While my parents and I were planning the wedding, Ralph was planning our honeymoon. It was a well-kept secret, even to me! He told me to pack for dress-up and for camping because we would do both. He told me that he was taking me to "The Land of Delight." I spent much time wondering where it was until we arrived at the cottage on Glen Lake, Leelanau County, Michigan, for the first week of our honeymoon. "Leelanau" translates from the Indian language to mean "Land of Delight." We canoed, swam, climbed sanddunes, and roamed the surrounding territory for the first week. We had what could have been a serious accident the second day of our marriage. I was driving on a slippery blacktop road when the car slid out of control and whirled into the ditch. Only the wheels were bent, and the week's stay allowed time for their repair. We proceeded to camp around the top of Lake Michigan and came home through Fond du Lac, Wisconsin, visiting Ralph's Uncle Johnny and Aunt Dixie. It was haymaking time and a farmer cannot stay away from the job indefinitely.

When we arrived at our future home it was vacant and ready for our residency. Mom and Dad Wier had moved to their new town house while we were on our honeymoon. We promptly ordered the delivery of the stove, refrigerator, bedroom suite, table and chairs we had picked out earlier, and set up housekeeping. I still remember the excitement and fun we had shopping for our first groceries. Mother Wier was wise enough to leave a few utensils and dishes. After a week we went back to Indiana to move my possessions. It was like any other pioneers moving west, only in a different era. Ralph loaded the big red farm truck with all my clothes, a rocking chair, my cedar chest full of linens and my piano on one side. On the other side Ralph had built a stall for my horse, Bonnie. Atop the whole load was my little one-horse sleigh! We made quite a spectacle heading toward the western prairie with Bonnie whinnying at every horse she saw! But we were in love and a whole new world was opening up ahead of us.

We got right down to work after our honeymoon. Ralph had a lot of farming to get caught up on. I started in on the garden Mother Wier and Ralph had planted for me. I also began redecorating our bedroom. We live in a big, old house, built partly in 1889 and partly in 1917. I did not especially like it when I came here to live, but I had no choice. It has ten rooms with ten-foot ceilings, but we started on it, redecorating a room at a time. Ralph is a clever carpenter and over the years we have remodeled much of it.

After we brought my horse from Indiana I rode her in the mornings while the men milked cows, then we ate our breakfast. Ralph and his Dad cared for between thirty and forty cows and after breakfast went to field work or whatever the day held for them. I had many rides on Bonnie exploring the timberlands near my new home. Often I would get almost lost but Old Blackie, the dog, or my horse could bring me home.

I loved the cove among the hills where we lived. Blackberry thickets, sassafras groves, and two pond areas made my journeys of exploration more adventurous. Creeks meandered down between hills. When Ralph and I would ride out to see the moonrise through the cedars we decided to name that spot Cedar Hill. Then he took me skiing on a steep slope such as you see in the movies. I named it Technicolor Hill. Later I would take our children over these same hills. Ralph built pond after pond until we now have six ponds, each named. They are to stop excessive runoff and conserve water. We finally arrived at a name for our farm, too. It was influenced by our love of horses, Double Horseshoe Farm. There have always been horses on this land and a pair of inverted horseshoes make our initial "W".

RALPH and DELIGHT WIER
LACON, ILLINOIS 61540
PHONE · AREA 309 246-8411

It wasn't too many years until we had this letterhead for our farm business. We used horseshoes freely in the decor of our house; candleholders, curtain tiebacks, and on the wall.

After redecorating the bedroom I undertook to brighten up the huge upstairs and downstairs hallways with the open staircase. We painted them bright red orange which Ralph's brother, Jack, dubbed the Hall of Flame. In later years after many little hands had fingered the stairway wall I had to paint a lot of big, bold white daisies with yellow centers and bright green leaves to cover the worst of the fingerprints. We called it our flowery pathway. The next room to come under the paintbrush was our dining room. The floral wallpaper was changed to dark green with chartruese dropped ceiling. We put maple furniture in that room where there are long double windows letting in the morning sunlight.

The remodeling process slowed somewhat a year-and-a-half later with the arrival of Rebecca. She was born in February, and soon we needed a nursery. Ralph had made her a hand-hewn walnut cradle to lie in during the daytime. Upstairs where we slept we prepared the girls' room, east off the big hall room. Ralph now strode with new purpose in his step. He was a family man!

We had great times with old friends, new friends, and neighbors. We housed them in the spare bedrooms upstairs. We also took parolees from St. Charles Reformatory during those early years. Pastor Mueller asked us to take one boy whom he knew needed just such a farm environment to straighten out his messed up life. These boys were sixteen years old, bad boys who had broken windows, robbed mailboxes, and needed discipline. In reality they needed love and a whole family, not one broken by fighting and divorce. Ralph had a strong right hand that he applied to the place that needed it. A spanking accomplished more than words. They knew we cared enough to do something about their actions. The rollicking good times popping corn, cracking nuts, swimming, hiking, and singing all involved them as integral part of our family. There was relief for their hurts.

A boy whose parents didn't have time for him told us that they gave him money and told him to go and spend it. He it was who enjoyed so much redecorating the west bedroom upstairs for his own. It involved brown paint for the walls, blue for the ceiling, and a border of apple trees. I made muslin curtains for the windows and trimmed them with rick-rack. The boy's pride became apparent and he stopped wetting his bed.

The coming of twins into our home was more than we could have hoped for. In the eighth month of my second pregnancy things were happening differently than before. There was too much action for one baby and I grew to a tremendous size. Upon our insistence that there were more than two elbows, feet, and knees poking up all over my abdomen the doctor took an X-ray that assured us we were right. Twins were on the way.

I hurried to order two layettes from Sears Roebuck. With Rebecca's things that should be enough. We made big plans for them. I was able to walk into the hospital. Daniel and David arrived totaling over fourteen pounds on July 14th.

Twins were fun and I nursed them until I ran out of milk. All along we had to give them bottles to satisfy their needs. I pitied the pioneer women who had twins and didn't have enough milk to feed them. Mother came and stayed three weeks helping me. There were diapers to wash, bottles to prepare, and Rebecca to care for. Mother and I enjoyed every minute of it, and Daddy wrote a poem about the boys. During the time Mother was here she threw out her diamond ring with the diaper water. We searched every spot we thought it could be, but we never found it. Daddy bought her a new one.

Once on a picnic when I was at a side table nursing the twins an Indian exchangee came to take my picture just to prove that women in this country were like those in his homeland. He was a married man with several children of his own and appreciated seeing babies nursed instead of bottle-fed. He believed bottle babies were weak babies.

The summer the twins were born we had Paul Cotroff, our Greek foreign student, and Lee, a parolee, living here and farming with Ralph. I remember Paul always took both basinettes and trudged up ahead with the twins while Rebecca walked beside me helping with the picnic basket to take food to the field and feed Daddy. Then there would be fishing, wiener roasting, or just plain picnicking while the men rested at noontime in the field. We were happy to be there with them and spend the restful hour. That was excitement enough for little Rebecca. She was willing to come home and go to her bed for afternoon naptime.

In Illinois on Double Horseshoe Farm there always were exciting things happening. I knew that if we were going to have a large family, the children would have to come close together. Ralph and I were both twenty-seven years old when we were married. Now, we were expecting our fourth child five years later. Timothy was born in October on Columbus Day. We were busy, but my goal was not to let all the work become drudgery. I needed to keep the sparkle in our lives that I knew should be there. A life of work need not be stifling. I started seeing small things along my path and giving thanks for them. There was little time for play, so work had to become fun. I told stories to the children while I ironed. We developed a story time which included some of our very own original tales. Rebecca was creative and helped think up plots, and the twins were old enough to chime in.

Maryanne came along one year later in October. A lady we had hired to help us through the last of my pregnancy and be here when we brought the new baby home said if she had been another boy she would have sent her back. But we had a red haired baby girl who was a real joy. All the boys loved her. Rebecca had a sister at last!

Now we had five children under five years of age. I hadn't realized it until one day my mother mentioned it. I was so busy doing for the family all day and night that we just took one day at a time. I wanted to marry a farmer, decorate and furnish a home, cook and sew and have children. The Lord had blessed us, but good!

We played, we laughed, we sang, and we worked. One snapshot shows Ralph on the floor in the evening with the twins and Timmy, all three, riding him like a horse.

As was our nightly custom, the children gathered around their father for family Bible-reading before bedtime. This photograph was taken in 1966, several months after Jonathan's birth.

It was a big happy family until tragedy struck our home. Danny was dead from getting caught in an auger. Ralph had gone to give blood at the bloodmobile, leaving the boys with the hired man. We called Ralph home and he rushed Danny to the hospital. The awful reality hit us that his legs were crushed. It was all over in a day and a half and we crept home to do what had to be done.

Now the fun was out of our life. I went around woodenly trying to care for the other children. I remember our doctor telling me I owed it to the other children to smile and be happy with them. Then I learned the dimension of real sympathy. Before, I had not known what loss felt like. Now I knew. I could relate to the hurting of the whole world.

We pulled ourselves along by helping others. Burying our grief in doing for others who were crippled as Danny would have been had he lived. We invited children to our farm. Danny died in March, and that summer we had three black and three white children from the inner-city school for exceptional children. They came for a week or two for a farm vacation they might never have had otherwise. We plunged into caring for them, wheelchair victims and all. One of them was jolly Judy, limping into our hearts as well as our lives. She endeared herself to our children, returning many years for visits. She gave us insight into a black girl's problems in a modern city.

It was in the following years before and after Paul was born that I was asked to speak about my awareness of everyday living and I accepted. About the same time the *Farm Journal* featured our kindergarten at home in one of their magazine issues. The reporter enjoyed a day with us as we busied ourselves with life on the farm.

Our experience with women living in our home at the time of Timmy's birth and again at Maryanne's birth proved that we had better go it alone. I managed nicely with help one day a week to clean the house. Baby Paul grew into our older children's hearts. I spent a lot of time with them in the playroom, and when I couldn't be there they taught Paul many of their little tricks.

I do have a conscience about work in a home, so I did all I could. I regret so many beautiful souls are frittering away their lives keeping their houses up with the Jonses when there are sunsets to see, paths to follow, cookies to bake, and people to cheer. In the Bible we read that not only the young but the old are capable of such inspiration. Caleb plowed new ground when he was asked what part of the land he would take for his reward after scouting in the promised land. He took to pioneering even though he was eighty-five years old.

Learning to be aware in the middle of work is what it is all about. It's the fourth dimension in living. Knowledge is the reservoir that feeds the stream of awareness. Awareness is the focusing lens that brings into sharp outline the beauties of everyday living. A poet will glimpse a deer and there comes a poem. James Watt watched the teakettle boil and invented the steam engine. Newton discovered the law of gravity from watching a falling apple. We all have vestiges of awareness, but the ability to see the familiar with clearer vision comes when we are able to share the experience with another.

Awareness begins in childhood. I remember homemade, fresh-ironed dresses Mother put on me every day for school. I felt like a princess in those dresses, favorite prints, plaids, and calicos she had made at her sewing machine. Now, looking back, I realize the feeling of well-being that I enjoyed came from the love that went into those clothes mother made, washed, starched, and ironed.

Awareness is for anyone who cultivates quality of mind and sensitivity of spirit. I believe golden agers are blessed with this more than anyone else. I pray I will be as aware as my mother is. Awareness grows with giving your best to those you love in an ever-expanding circle. It isn't something to do after the work is all done. It is best cultivated in the midst of work.

David and his bride, Julie, smile happily on their wedding day, September 17, 1977, at the United Methodist Church in Dayton, Indiana. Julie's parents are Mr. and Mrs. Donald Miller of rural La Fayette, Indiana.

In years gone by, it was too often accepted that only people of means had the opportunity to enjoy the finer things in life. Only the nobility could enjoy the fine arts of music, painting, writing, and drama. They were not allowed to turn their hands to work. I pity them because they were denied the refreshed feeling of making useful crafts that make our homes liveable. It's small wonder we ordinary people became so capable at cooking, weaving, quilting, crocheting, embroidery, and other handicrafts.

Paul and Nancy were married December 15, 1979, at St. John's Lutheran Church in Varna, Illinois. They were both juniors at Illinois State University at the time. Nancy's parents are Mr. and Mrs. Donald Johnson of Varna.

I used to read stories to the children. One particular one bears repeating. It is about the poor family that appreciated the dinner of stew because the mother could tell her children that the onions were silver, the potatoes were ivory, and the carrots were gold. The outlook made all the difference in the world. When there was soup for dinner I used to hold the children up so they could peer into the kettle and see the iridescent bubbles shimmering across the surface of the soup.

We made up happy little stories. The outstanding ones I copied down as the children helped me dream them up while I was ironing in the playroom. Rebecca was the dreamer and the oldest. She thought Honey Bear was a good name for David and Blue Bear was a good name for Tim. The rest we left to our imagination.

The busy years flew by, with farm, church, and community involvements. All of our children became active in 4-H and scouting. They were happy musicians. They worked with pets, livestock, cleaned their rooms sometimes, baked cookies, said prayers at bedtime, and grew up. I had always wanted to adopt a child to give another child a better chance in life. Ralph answered my request with another child of our own. Jonathan came into our lives seven years after the others and brought all the bonuses that a little life can bring to a family. He was a rare pleasure, although some people thought I must be his grandmother. When he was born I celebrated my forty-third birthday in the hospital.

Our six busy youngsters were in all sorts of activities, making our life full to brimming over. But the world stopped suddenly one night at sundown when Maryanne was instantly electrocuted in a farm accident. She tripped over a low electric fence that had been erected to keep raccoons from eating our sweet corn. All the impossible possibilities accumulated to stop her heart. She was playing happily in a wet cornfield after a rain, chasing her brothers. She fell with the wire across her chest and both arms. The doctor explained that the voltage pulsed at the same time as her heartbeat and stopped it.

I could not understand why automobiles still went up the road. Everything in me had stopped. I refused reality as I refused food, but we went through the sad preparations as we had for Danny. Tears flowed afresh when people came. Oh, the ache, the numbing ache deep inside that wouldn't let us sleep. I know, now, the very work of preparing for a funeral is good to dull the shock. Maryanne, who had just been teaching little three-year-old Jonathan to sing, was gone.

Putting up her violin, giving away her clothing, closing her collection of poetry and her Bible all were attended to. Months passed when I felt no joy in living. I might lose another child! What was the use to go on! That was where I was when I found my Savior. Underneath were the everlasting arms. I had never needed to use them, trust them. I had enjoyed energy to spare, enthusiasm in abundance, good things to fill my lifetime, but now they couldn't make me go on. I let go of it all and let God take my life and do with it whatever He wanted. I stepped out of the way and let Him finally be my master.

It didn't happen all in a day, although I know the date, time, and place it started. We had opened our church in late February to several Christian laymen for a witness mission to bring new life and vigor to our people. Praise the Lord, it came to me in the form of a little booklet that started guiding my prayer life. Daily I prayed "Nothing I have is my own . . . . I am a given person . . . . I want to renew my vow daily to serve You to the best of my ability, loving person after person 24 hours a day." And He did hear me and forgive me, the sinner that I am, and He did heal me to be a channel for Him.

Now I can truthfully say, no two days are ever alike. By getting my marching orders from Him in the morning I receive new inspiration daily to serve Him. It may be for quiet days when I have had only Ralph and the kids to grow impatient toward. He gives me patience. It may be for big days when the pace is dizzying and I would not know which thing to do first. He sorts out my priorities and tells me that first things must come first. I look at children in Sunday school class as possibilities for Him. I give our own children over to Him daily and ask Him to guide them. I hadn't done a very good job by myself.

It was a hard lesson to learn, but finally I realized that all my dearest ones weren't here with us. Heaven seemed nearer and dearer. I wanted to find more truths in the Bible to direct my life. Jesus said, "Do unto others . . . ." It led me to want to share my faith the best way I knew how—in our home. Always a person to enjoy people, now I was being a channel for the Lord. I would do more peoplekeeping than house-keeping.

I noticed the children enjoyed visitors in our home. We worked together to share what we had with whomever came, and we were the blessed. We had always had an interest in foreign students and have had them from every continent in the world. They opened exotic doors to their native cultures we would never otherwise have experienced. But we now were open to those hurting individuals, parolees, drug addicts, and child abuse victims. We brought more of them into our home and they showed us first hand the hurts that accompany the ills of our society. The farm was to some extent the remedy for their ailments, but I knew it had to be more than fresh air, sunshine, and good food; it had to be Jesus.

We shared our home with inner-city children; children on farm vacations who were here not only because they needed our environment, they needed our Christian heritage. They came from broken homes, broken houses, broken morals, broken environments. LOVE was the main ingredient we fed them on. Around our dinner table we first showed love toward them so that the food they ate could heal their bodies. Ralph likes to sit at our table and talk with those young people who come, disturbed, perplexed by life. We let them tell us what hurts and then we love them in response.

Henry David Thoreau said, "Find your strength in solitude." When a visitor comes and Jon wants to sit and watch TV with him, the first impulse Ralph has is to get them both outdoors doing chores. There has been little time for the media to subvert the minds of our children. We know our Lord wants us to have quiet time so He can speak to us. We cannot open others' minds but we can set up the situation for it to happen. That situation is certainly not with radio, TV, or blaring tapes.

Another rule we have made for our lives is so simple we stand to be ridiculed for it, but it works. We give eight hours for sleep to restore our minds and bodies so we can do the strenuous day's tasks. We thank the Lord for good health. We are the temples of the Lord so we must care for our bodies. Good health habits are of primary importance. We do not wish anyone in our home to take anything into their bodies that will alter the divine plan of its working, thinking, feeling, and breathing components. My father was a puritan. I have inherited it straight from Mom and Dad. Ralph, by the same token, grew up in a conservative family who believed in the simple, rigorous life. We are only living the way we have been taught. We swerve neither to the left nor to the right.

Our faith has taught us that we must give the Lord opportunity to heal us. Jesus moved apart from the throngs. We, too, must go apart. It is the original version of not keeping up with the Joneses.

Now it is coming to the surface that the cause of American teenagers malnutrition is no guidance at home. Mothers have the well being of their families in their hands. The kitchen is the laboratory and she is the technician. It is a frightening responsibility, but taken one day at a time with the Lord, you cannot fail.

Ralph and I beam proudly in the midst of our rapidly expanding family circle. In this photograph taken after Paul and Nancy's wedding are (front row, left to right): Ralph, Jennifer Lynn, me, and Jonathan. Second row: Timothy and Sandy Wier with son, Levi Alan, David and Julie Wier, Paul and Nancy Wier, Dale and Rebecca Locke with son, Andrew John.

Then when we become genuinely ill, we have strong bodies to submit to medical doctors for their help. We have had our share of illnesses. Because of the hazards of farming, Ralph has had his nose severed, a vertebra cracked, and numerous stitches from various accidents. Our children have been in surgery, too. Tim was operated on for slipped epiphesis of both hip joints. He submitted as willingly as a twelve-year-old could, and cheerfully bore himself on crutches for months. Jon had a relocation of his right shoulder joint from damage at birth. We have not been spared the trauma of the knife. We have had God's healing hand perform miracles through doctors and without doctors.

Our faith is growing daily. Tuesday evening sees us gathered around the dining room table with friends who want to pursue the Word and apply it in their lives. Our children, seeing Bible study in our home, have looked for it on college campuses. They became involved in very real witnessing and brought home to us their inspiration.

An old minister told me one time when I asked him about the lack of witnessing in our modern way of life: "First, you have to have something to witness about!"

Could it be possible that good people go to church Sunday after Sunday worshipping in churches all over our land and have nothing to witness about? Wake up America!

Part III

Candies, Snacks, Drinks

There are many decors for kitchens. Ours features displays of the children's projects. The refrigerator and freezer have been decorated with artwork from young accomplishments for years. It is surprising how children try harder if they know their attempts are going to be displayed. And for a little spice in life I have a trivet above my stove saying, "Love, like coffee, should be made fresh every morning." It doesn't hurt marital relations to show some love in the kitchen. Charity begins at home.

I have just finished sweeping up the piles of dirt from many boots and much activity over the weekend. We had a houseful of youth. I was thinking about those kids playing games in the living room. There were eight of them. I dished up Cherry Delight, popped corn, and put oranges in a bowl while Ralph got out candy and nuts.

Josef, the Polish farm trainee living with us, had a French trainee, Ives, visiting. We greatly enjoyed the conversation with these visitors from other cultures and the sharing of our David's last night at home before going back to second semester of his senior college year. I savored the moments around the table together.

It was with a kind of delightful abandon that we opened our doors on New Year's Day. Skates flung by the fireplace, forty people at a buffet. Friends, relatives, and neighbors helped make a really happy New Year. Our sleep that night was sweet and deep!

When Danny died twenty years ago I decided that I

would never again be carefree. I solemnly told Ralph this fact and he agreed. When Maryanne died nine years ago we reaffirmed that fact. The revelation from the Holy Spirit was that we needn't be carefree to abandon ourselves wholly to the Lord's guidance. This was a long and painful discovery but it happened.

We had hoped after Danny died to build a children's home, a refuge for youngsters, across the road in the wooded hills on our farm. We were warned against it at every turn. Too expensive, too much personnel needed, nurse on duty, doctor on call, not to be approved by state authorities, not even approved by our church conference! They wanted in-family experience for their orphans and not another children's home, an institution to take the place of the home.

After eighteen years the wisdom of their decision comes and abides with us. We are cleaning up after another weekend retreat of young people living within our home. Not being exclusive nor choosing youngsters, we have foreigners, blacks, orphan kids from the community who like farm life, kids from the inner city who need to experience farming environs, itinerant college youth wandering around to find themselves, students of economics, atomic energy, nursing, mathematics, agriculture—they are all welcome. Even cross-country horseback riders found our farm the summer of 1975, and we let them bathe and eat and sleep before they saddled up and went on their way next day.

I see in sweeping up the back porch that our desire to be a home for youth has been answered. We may never again be carefree. Responsibility does not grow on the carefree soul. Only those who learn that "His yoke is easy; His burden is light" can open their home with delightful confidence that they are doing the will of their Lord.

Although children have a special place in our hearts, a most-welcome guest will always be Aunt Lessie. When she comes to visit us, Melba Noble usually comes, too. She was here at maple syrup time and since she is a candy maker, she took home some of our maple syrup and used it in her candies. Here are her recipes.

Maple Nut Fudge

1 tablespoon butter
1 cup sugar
½ cup maple syrup
⅓ cup cream
1 cup chopped walnuts
   or pecans (optional)
¼ teaspoon salt

Melt butter in saucepan, add sugar, syrup, and cream; stir until sugar is dissolved. Bring to boiling point and boil without stirring at 238°F, or until mixture forms a soft ball when tried in cold water. Remove candy from fire, and let it stand undisturbed until cool. Add nuts and salt, beat with a wooden spoon or pour out on marble slab and work with spatula until candy begins to get firm. Turn immediately into a buttered pan or spread between candy bars and mark in squares. Melba uses this recipe for bonbon centers. After working mixture until it creams, she then shapes into small bars and dips in melted chocolate coating.

She includes variations of this basic recipe in Maple Chocolate Fudge in which she omits the nuts and salt and adds 2 squares unsweetened chocolate and ½ teaspoon of vanilla. She uses these for bonbon centers, also dipped in butterscotch coating.

Her Maple Marshmallow Fudge is the same basic recipe omitting the nuts and salt. When the fudge begins to get firm, return it to the saucepan to melt. Pour half of the mixture in a ¼" layer in a buttered pan. Lay on it a layer of miniature marshmallows, cover with remaining fudge and leave until firm. Cut in ¾" squares.

Her Pralines are from the same basic recipe, too. Make recipe for Maple Nut Fudge. When mixture becomes firm, put in saucepan, stir over hot water until softened, and add nuts, preferably pecans, in large pieces. Drop from spoon onto waxed paper in rounds 3" in diameter. This is the easiest praline recipe I have seen.

Kids' Maple Candy

Our children made their maple candy, too. They had a recipe that was sure every time. They started with a package of cream cheese and a couple tablespoons of maple syrup. They blended in enough powdered sugar to form patties. Into each small patty they pressed a nut. Sometimes they rolled them into balls for a nut surprise. It is easy and never stays around long enough to grow stale.

❧

Caramel Corn can be made with maple syrup, too, by substituting it for the white syrup. We used to take a half bushel of caramel corn to church family nights and the people loved it. The janitor had the remains to sweep up, but the kids remember those nights fondly and tell me about them now. I used to pour the hot mixture over the corn and rush to church. I boiled equal parts white sugar and maple syrup till it spun a thread, then added a dash of salt and a bit of vinegar to crackle it. But here is a surefire recipe that will not stick to your teeth or pull out a filling.

Caramel Corn

8 cups popped corn
2 cups light brown sugar
½ cup white syrup
½ pound margarine
¼ teaspoon soda

Boil together five minutes then add ¼ teaspoon soda. Pour over corn and mix well. Place in shallow pan, well greased, and bake 1 hour at 200°. Stir every 15 minutes. I cut the margarine to 2 tablespoons for weight watchers and add salt. Artificial butter salt is acceptable, too.

Chocolate Popcorn

4 quarts popped corn
3½ tablespoons cocoa
1 cup sugar, pinch of salt
½ cup milk
1½ tablespoons butter
½ teaspoon vanilla
½ teaspoon soda

Blend cocoa, sugar, and milk and cook to 275° on candy thermometer. Stir in butter, vanilla, and soda. Pour over popped corn and blend. Spread on cookie sheets to separate. Now you've heard everything in recipes. Doris Lock gave the recipe to Rebecca. It is a gourmet treat.

Easy Fudge

1 can Eagle Brand milk
1 12-ounce package
   sweet chocolate bits
1 stick margarine
12 graham crackers

Crush crackers in bread bag with a rolling pin. Melt margarine, chocolate bits, and condensed milk together on stove. Stir in graham crackers to which may be added chopped nuts. Press into buttered 9" x 13" pan or smaller, depending on desired thickness. Cool and cut in squares. My girls were making candy for their dad for Father's Day and hit upon this recipe for which Ralph has a weakness.

Jonathan's Candy

1 package chocolate chips
or
1 package butterscotch chips
2 cans chow mein noodles

Melt chips in double boiler and pour over noodles spread evenly on a buttered baking sheet. Jonathan proudly made these when he was in second grade and we gobbled them up.

Darlene's Fudge Pops

3-ounce package of chocolate pudding
⅓ cup sugar
3 cups milk
1 cup cream or canned milk

Cook as regular pudding. When done add the one cup cream and pour into popsicle molds and freeze. Makes 16 "lickin good" treats everybody likes. Darlene Pieper of Hammond, Illinois, gave this recipe to me. Jonathan begs for them each summer.

❧

Gelatine blocks make a chewy, non-messy snack for our children. A schoolteacher I knew filled blown eggs with the gelatin mixture for Easter eggs.

Knox Blocks

4 packages unflavored gelatine
3 packages fruit-flavored gelatine
4 cups boiling water

Dissolve the two types of gelatine mixed together with the boiling water added slowly. Pour into a 9″ x 13″ pan. Cut in squares when set. They can be picked up and eaten with fingers.

Maple Syrup Steamer

1 cup hot milk
1 to 2 tablespoons maple syrup
½ teaspoon butter

We like our product so we have developed a company drink when visitors come, serving steamers rich with butter. This drink can also be served without butter. For health food enthusiasts, blackstrap molasses can be substituted.

Grandma's Whole Grape Juice

I have nearly a hundred quarts of this whole grape juice in my cellar now waiting to strengthen Ralph for his rigorous daily grind throughout the year. The theory that the fruits of your own region are the best for you supports my making a large quantity of grape juice and not wasting an ounce of the precious stuff.

I fill each jar with washed, whole grapes to the ¾ mark. I put ½ cup of sugar and add boiling water to seal. Process in hot water bath 10 minutes to insure airtight closure. It contains the vitamins necessary to cure colds in winter. It has contributed to the recuperation of children who were weak and needed its strengthening; it is canned sunshine.

༄

When David gets up early and wants an eyeopener, or at night when he needs something to fill the empty corner of his stomach, he makes Orange Julius.

Orange Julius

½ of 6-ounce can frozen
   orange concentrate
½ cup milk
½ cup water
¼ cup sugar
½ teaspoon vanilla
5 or 6 ice cubes,
   crushed coarsely

Combine all ingredients in blender container; cover and blend until smooth, about 30 seconds. Serve immediately. Makes about 3 cups.

I like to drink the kind of tea which goes all the way back to the Adams family of Revolutionary days. Here is a recipe that would have spiced things up a bit in Boston harbor. Rebecca and I came upon this spicy and refreshing drink that can be stored in a dry state and used as needed.

Spicy Tea

¾ **cup instant tea**
2 **cups orange-flavored instant breakfast drink**
3 **ounces (1 package) lemonade mix**
1½ **cups sugar**
2 **teaspoons cinnamon**
1 **teaspoon ground cloves**
¼ **teaspoon salt**

Combine ingredients. Store in tightly sealed container. To serve, stir 2 heaping teaspoons of mix into each cup of boiling water. Makes about 4½ cups of mix.

❧

A hearty drink hot or cold is eggnog. It is good for people who are in training or recuperating from an illness. It also uses good, wholesome farm products and is excellent for children.

Egg Nog

4 **eggs**
½ **teaspoon salt**
½ **cup sugar**
4 **cups milk**
vanilla or nutmeg

Combine in blender the above ingredients using vanilla or chocolate flavoring for cold and nutmeg or maple syrup for hot drinks. Our visiting inner-city children taught us to put shell and all in when we broke the eggs. They had parents who knew the value of calcium.

One of the advantages of having a flock of laying hens, bantams, or maybe ducks (we have Muscovy ducks) is that these birds all provide the main ingredient for deviled eggs. I fall back on that versatile dish as a side treat for many meals and take it to potlucks. Deviled eggs go with any food you prepare.

Canning, Preserving

I have been a gardener since I was in diapers. I remember Dad and Mother taking me along to plant, cultivate, and harvest fruits and vegetables that made up most of our daily food. It was not always willingly that I went to the garden. Nevertheless, I have gone to great pains to offer our own children the same experience because over the years I realize how much gardening has meant to me.

Like many conservationists today, I am 100 percent sure the knowledge of how to grow our own food and reap it from the soil can save our lives in times of need. I intend to teach our children so they can teach my grandchildren all that my parents taught me.

Unwillingly I have hoed rows of vegetables, swatted potato bugs into buckets, sweated through corn husking, pea shelling and cherry pitting, only to learn that is the way to health. "Garden fresh" is as delicious as it sounds.

At first I thought the boisterous children were an unnecessary nuisance in my green sanctuary, but now I brag about our kids using the cabbages for stools and riding their trikes up and down the rows. I put the baby in a cardboard box beside me as I weeded in early summer. The baby liked that so much better than staying in the baby buggy because he could tip over the box and finger the dirt when my back was turned. Rebecca had naps under mosquito netting in the blackberry briars while Ralph and I sweated and swatted mosquitos, picking the luscious large fruits.

I often have had to beg for weeding help from teen-agers. The most effective method is (after a rain that has softened the soil) to have Ralph announce to the whole family, "Everybody take a row and weed it all the way." How they'd scramble to get the easy bean or onion rows while we got the carrot or mixed flower rows.

I've had produce plopped on my kitchen table to sur-prise me when I didn't want to see another vegetable after canning all day. The family thinks canning is syn-onymous with the word "mother." The payoff comes when company arrives and I open jars of food from my storage shelves. The hearty approval flatters me.

I'm not being fooled, however, remembering the toil over a hot stove during the hottest days of summer. It's just that my priorities line up to testify that conserving money and the best food our soil can produce makes good sense. Besides, gardening teaches kids discipline and a work ethic that is one of the most valuable lessons in life.

Lorene McCully has been my nearest neighbor, raising her children just ahead of ours, coming to let them play with ours, sharing recipes and her good fruit and vegetables when we didn't have some of the same. Her husband Frank would pick apples to bring to us before our apple orchard started yielding. She gave me this recipe that I will share with you.

Lorene's Tomato Soup

(3 pints)

1 gallon tomatoes, cut in quarters
2 pieces of celery, diced
1 onion, chopped
¼ green pepper, chopped
3 whole cloves
small bay leaf
dash of thyme
¼ teaspoon chili powder
dash oregano

Cook all together and put through sieve.

½ cup sugar
½ cup flour
2 tablespoons salt

Mix last three ingredients with water for white sauce. Add to sieved vegetables. Heat, bringing to boil. Pour in sterilized pint jars. Seal and place in hot water bath 10 minutes. (I always double this recipe for a most delicious soup base, spaghetti sauce base, or any other tomato sauce need. It competes favorably with the commercial products.

Home-canned Vegetables for Soup

My readers ask about my recipe for canning vegetables together for vegetable soup. I use what I have from my garden, and often have to make it when the heads of cabbage are ready. But I have stored away a few green beans, limas, or a head of cabbage to wait till I have the right amount of ripe tomatoes.

164

Slice and cut fine vegetables needing the longest cooking first and place them in a large pan with 2 to 4 cups of water. I vary quantities year by year, but start with a couple dozen carrots. Then I add a head or two of chopped cabbage. You might want more than 8 or 10 onions, depending on size. Next come the green beans cut small, or green baby limas, whichever you have. A couple quarts of them will suffice. After that scald and peel 20, more or less, tomatoes. Preserving all the juice, chop these over the simmering mixture. I have been adding all the vegetables to the pan while it is simmering on the stove so the firmest vegetables have simmered longest. Stir well and heat the mixture thoroughly to wilt the vegetables. I do not add potatoes or meat stock. I always have these when I want to prepare the soup for the table.

In scalded hot jars add 1 teaspoon of salt per quart of vegetables. Close lids and pressure-cook the length of time for the firmest vegetables. This provides mixed vegetables our family likes all in one jar when we are hungry for homemade, hot vegetable soup. I usually add it to beef broth and chop potatoes into it, seasoning it to taste.

For a long time I pondered over what the commercial canneries put into their soups that make them tasty. Then I read my herb chart and started experimenting. Rebecca had a hobby of raising herbs, and Aunt Murrie added to our collection. Our neighbor, Johanna Casey, shared some of her oregano, geranium, and sage to add to the rosemary, garlic, and chives I grow. Dill has always been in my garden. Mother always raises it, too. Mint can take over a corner of the farm, but I'm willing to take that risk just to have it to smell.

Tomato Sauce

Sieve Italian tomatoes after scalding. For each quart of tomato puree add:

¾ cup minced onion

½ teaspoon dried oregano leaves

2 teaspoons salt

½ teaspoon garlic powder

½ teaspoon dried basil leaves

½ teaspoon sugar

dash of pepper

Bring combined ingredients to a boil; reduce to simmer for 1 hour, covered. Process in jars with hot water bath for 15 minutes. Rebecca makes her own sauce every year.

❧

My sister-in-law, Florence Wier, shared with me her chili sauce recipe. I often make a batch of it and a batch of blender catsup for a smoother product.

Chili Sauce

1 gallon tomatoes, chopped

2 big onions, chopped

1 cup celery, chopped

3 red peppers, chopped

5 cloves

1 cup vinegar

1 cup brown sugar

2 teaspoons salt

1 stick cinnamon

5 peppercorns (or to taste)

Cook together until thickened, stirring often to prevent scorching. Can immediately, after lifting out cinnamon, cloves, and peppercorns.

Blender Ketchup

48 medium tomatoes
2 ripe sweet peppers
2 sweet green peppers
4 onions
3 cups vinegar
3 cups sugar
3 tablespoons salt
1½ tablespoons allspice
3 tablespoons dry mustard
1½ teaspoons cloves
1½ teaspoons cinnamon
½ teaspoon hot red pepper

Quarter tomatoes, remove stem ends. Add peppers, seeded and cut in strips, and onions, peeled and quartered. Mix.

Put vegetables in blender container, filling jar ¼ full. Blend at high speed 4 seconds. Pour into large kettle. Repeat until all vegetables are blended.

Add vinegar, sugar, salt, and spices tied loosely in a thin muslin bag. Simmer, uncovered, in slow oven, 325°, or in an electric saucepan until volume is reduced one-half. Remove spices. Seal immediately in hot jars. Makes 5 pints.

Spiced Pears

1 cup light corn syrup
1 cup sugar
½ cup vinegar
2 cups water
8 fresh pared and cored pears
2 sticks cinnamon
1 tablespoon allspice
1 teaspoon cloves
2 strips lemon rind
⅛ teaspoon red food coloring
⅛ teaspoon green food coloring

Mix all ingredients except food colorings. Bring to boil and simmer 15 minutes uncovered. Strain out spices. Divide liquid in 2 parts. Add red to one part and green to other. Simmer and add pears. Simmer 5 minutes, basting frequently. When finished with all pears, return them to syrup to cool. Rebecca gives these delicious pears for Christmas gifts when we have an ample crop in our fall harvest.

Pear Relish

Sometimes in the fall when we have many firm Kieffer pears this recipe is a fine one to use them up. Especially good for potlucks and Thanksgiving dinners.

8 quarts of pears
2 packages cranberries
3 oranges
3 cups sugar
2 teaspoons salt

Quarter pears; do not peel. Cut out centers and grind quarters with cranberries and oranges. Simmer 20 minutes with sugar and salt added. This may be canned. Store in a dark place so the color will not fade.

We go round the calendar with our homemade treats. Canned apple cider is just about the best taste one can have with a pork dinner. It can be preserved when it is inexpensive or made at home in the fall. Homemade apple butter is another treat you cannot afford to miss. It makes great Christmas gifts, also. Gone are the days of the open kettle apple butter making when Grandpa presided with the stirring paddle and the women pared apples all morning. But Mother still makes delicious apple butter. Here is her recipe.

Oven Apple Butter

1 gallon of thick applesauce
1 cup of cider (vinegar can be used if no cider is
    on hand)
2 to 3 pounds sugar, depending on the tartness
    of the apples
½ teaspoon cinnamon, to suit taste

In a roaster place applesauce and cider. Cook in the oven for an hour stirring occasionally, at 300°. Add sugar and continue to bake until thick and glossy, stirring to keep from sticking. Lastly add cinnamon to suit taste. It will take 3 to 4 hours to complete it. Seal in hot jars at once. To save oven from being splattered, place aluminum foil on roaster. Punch holes in foil to allow for evaporation.

Mother also was an expert at jam and jelly making. She and Dad put away several kinds of preserves, but most unique have been her gooseberry preserves and her currant jam and jelly. I have worked out a few newer recipes from necessity. Some years there were no grapes or currants or gooseberries or strawberries. My jelly eaters demanded something. I substituted yummy rhubarb jam. Now I have to make it for its unusual taste to satisfy the family's demands. Sometimes I add rhubarb to strawberry or pineapple to extend them. Shortages or not, there never is a shortage of rhubarb. We have heard it said that rhubarb is good for what ails you. Rhubarb jam on toast makes a winter morning taste like spring.

Unfailing Rhubarb Jam

2 pounds finely chopped rhubarb (4 cups)
2 cups water
1 box Sure-Jell
5½ cups sugar

Combine rhubarb with 2 cups water. Heat just to boiling. Add Sure-Jell and sugar. Bring mixture to a rolling boil and boil 1 minute. Test with 2-drop method for doneness. Pour into 7 sterilized 8-ounce jelly glasses.

❧

Elderberry jelly has become so popular that there is a recipe printed in pectin books for it. I always add apple juice, lemon juice, or vinegar to it. But Uncle Kirby at Folk Valley takes the prize for making unusual kinds of jelly. This year he gave us rose hip jelly and gave Rebecca wild plum jelly. Here is his own pectin base recipe.

Homemade Pectin

To be used for strawberry, cherry, rhubarb, pineapple, plum, grape, and elderberry jellies.

10 pounds whole crabapples cut in quarters

Boil in kettle with water barely covering. Mash with a potato masher after 30 minutes. Run through colander, then through jelly bag which is allowed to hang overnight. Boil again to half of the volume. Seal for future use. (For crabapple jelly it can be taken down 1/6.)

When needed:

½ cup apple pectin
4 cups low pectin fruit

Follow usual sugar proportions. Bring to boil, test after 1 minute for 2 drops forming on the edge of a spoon.

Amelia's Pickles

Put medium and small cucumbers in brine of 1 pint salt and 1 gallon water. Leave 7 days. Drain off brine and cover pickles with boiling water with 1 tablespoon of alum added. Drain off second day and cover again with boiling water with ½ tablespoon alum added. Next day drain off and cover with a syrup made of 6 pints of vinegar and 12 cups sugar. Split each pickle. Every day for 3 days drain off syrup, heat hot, pour over pickles. Add 1 cup sugar each day but do not add sugar on last day. Pack pickles in jars and cover with hot liquid. This much sugar and vinegar will do a large batch of pickles. (Our kids enjoy them straight from the stone jar, so I don't can all of them.) When canning be sure to seal, placing in hot water bath 10 minutes.

Mustard Pickles

1 cup sugar
1 cup salt
1 cup mustard, powdered
2 quarts vinegar
1 gallon cucumbers

For this recipe you may use uncut medium to large cucumbers. Pour mixture of spices and sugar on cold. Do not heat. Add 1 cup of water to vinegar if it seems strong. Put in glass jars or in a stone jar for 3 weeks.

Then sample. Dad and I used to go down to the cellar and fish out a mustard pickle in August and eat it beside the stone jar while we were cooling off.

For years when our children were small Mother kept us in pickles. I didn't have time to do pickling and had very little luck making them. Then I realized that I could never learn younger and tackled Mother's pickling recipes. Her Chow Chow recipe was Daddy's favorite. We still make it every fall from last of the garden vegetables. It is a relish that makes hot dogs delectable. It is automatically packed along with ketchup and mustard for wiener roasts.

Chow Chow
or
Green Tomato Relish

1 peck green tomatoes
4 green peppers
4 red peppers
2 cups chopped celery
½ cup salt
2 cups minced onion
3 cups vinegar
2 cups sugar
½ cup celery seed

Grind together the above vegetables and let stand overnight with salt added. Drain thoroughly. Bring the seasonings to boil and add vegetables. Pack in boiled jars, seal.

Many people use "boughten" horseradish to spark up their pork dishes, but you readily can make your own. I raise the roots in our garden alongside the rhubarb plants. Dig early, just after the first green leaves come up to show where the plants are.

Horseradish

6 roots of horseradish, little finger-sized
  (or equivalent)
6 roots of parsnip (same amount as
  horseradish)
1 teaspoon salt (vary to taste)
½ cup water
½ cup sugar (vary to taste)
¼ cup vinegar

Cut horseradish and parsnips into small pieces and drop one by one into blender in which water and vinegar have been placed. Start and stop blender with each addition until a finely chopped white texture has been reached. Season with sugar and salt to taste. Take care during the process that you do not inhale deeply. Burns have been caused by horseradish in its pure state. This recipe will keep indefinitely. I usually make up only a pint at a time and keep in tightly closed container because it will lose flavor and go into other foods kept nearby.

When I came to live in Illinois no one ever heard of sweet sauerkraut, nor did the ladies of our community make beet-pickled eggs. I was raised on these delicacies since I grew up in a German community. We always had extra cabbage heads sometime during the growing season so they went into the big stone jar in the basement for sauerkraut. Mother and Dad used to make it with just enough salt to track a rabbit and it turned out delicious. I found when I tried to make it that the right amount of salt was hard to determine. Then I found a recipe which I have followed carefully with good results.

Stone Jar Sauerkraut

Shred and salt 5 pounds of cabbage at a time. To each 5 pounds of cabbage add 3½ tablespoons of pure granulated salt, not iodized. Pack each layer firmly and evenly so juice begins to rise. A potato masher works fine. Do not pound cabbage, but by the time you are finished juice should cover cabbage.

Cover with a couple layers of clean white cloth, tucking in the edges. Weigh it down with a clean plate and a glass jar filled with water. Juice should come over the plate.

Fermentation takes about 3 weeks at 70° temperature. Remove film or mold and scald cover cloth as needed. When bubbling stops, fermentation has ended. Tap jar to see if any bubbles rise. Pack in clean quart jars to within an inch of the top. Cover with juice. You may need to make more juice from a weak brine (1½ tablespoon salt to 1 quart water).

Set jars in cold water to necks and bring slowly to boil. Put on lids and process in boiling water bath 30 minutes.

Mother and I have talked a lot about nature's remedies. Rebecca has had an herb garden since she was a little girl. We all know there are benefits in natural foods. There are also other benefits, such as growing garlic near beans and other vegetables plagued by bugs. Bugs don't like onions or any of the rest of the onion family. Marigolds and nasturtiums are also a boon to a vegetable garden, protecting other plants by their odor.

My mother and father used to eat dandelions in the spring for a tonic. I still dig the little beasties out of the yard to put with browned bacon gravy and chopped onion. When salt and vinegar are added and the chopped dandelions are stirred in to lightly wilt, they are delicious. Mrs. Boyles, however, boils her greens and crumbles bacon strips with vinegar over them.

Ralph and I like to gather watercress from the springs down by the river on cold days in early February. Everything else is covered with snow. There in the spring water grows verdantly green watercress. It looks like a miracle. It sparks salads with its peppery flavor. Pick it early because it grows more bitter as springtime develops.

We feel like the pioneers must have felt in spring when they went to the timber to dig sassafras roots. We always have a few cups of sassafras tea for another spring tonic.

Horseradish roots are dug early, too, and prepared with parsnips for dressing pork and vegetables. I used to cry over the job of grinding them even out on the back porch. Now I do it, a little at a time, in the blender. It turns out creamy white. It needs salt, sugar, and vinegar and some parsnip to make it milder. Pure horseradish can burn skin, so beware!

All year long we go to the timber for taste treats. We find wild asparagus, tender poke shoots, and tangy mustard greens. Wild strawberries follow soon after to treat the tastebuds to a rare flavor, and then wild goose-berries, which may be used green or ripened.

"Cherries are ripe" sing the birds and children in July. We flock over to pick the two trees before the birds get them. Years ago we used to take the children with us up to Deer Island and pick a crate of blackberries large as your finger around. I canned quarts of them and made jam. Mother Wier came and picked them for jelly, but now they are gone. The deciduous trees grew up in their thickets of briars as is the plan of nature, and our cattle have grazed away their low starts.

Wild raspberries grow up the road gulleys and supply enough for taste treats and jam. Then the fruits in our orchard take over, supplying our table all the way through fall, progressing from peaches, apples, pears, and going on through grapes and late pears and apples.

Along the way there are elderberries to gather for gift jelly. Some years I have made red haw jelly. Other years I've made wild cherry jelly or wild grape jelly with its bitter-tart taste.

Kitchen Crafts, Natural Remedies

Children have come to our family and blessed it. We are grateful. It hurts me to see or hear about unwanted children.

Some say that a child cannot repay his cost. How do they judge the important things in life? Our children have been preparing to do their life's work ever since they had toy workbenches, dishes, pots, pans, ironing boards, brooms, and dolls. The boys always preferred to play with Ralph's tools rather than with their own toys. The girls seemed to like sewing real clothing better than doll clothes. We had a playroom where toys had to be cleared away at the end of play. In our "nursery school" at the kitchen table, the children had cleanup time at the close of their playdough or coloring sessions.

Before we knew it, they were old enough to be Brownies and Cub Scouts. Then they had new crafts along with their school projects. They had pets to care for before they earned badges. They had cookies to learn to bake for treats. The project may not have been new, but the incentive was and they went into scouting and 4-H with zest. They learned that their leaders wanted them to excel, as their parents had taught them to do.

Grandparents were important at this phase of our children's lives. They were glad to do for grandma or grandpa what they might drag their feet over doing for mom and dad. Somehow, grandparents reward their grandchildren in such nice ways—homemade cookies or a trip to the zoo. Children need rewards as do any other little creatures.

The children were soon old enough to help daily with farm chores. It was great for awhile; the ingenuity on the part of parents had to be applied to keep them willing to feed lambs their bottles, calves their buckets of milk, chickens their feed; to gather the eggs, and carry in wood for the fireplace. I have never had any child do any particular chore, like burning trash, regularly unless he wanted to do it. I have usually assisted with the job, done it myself part of the time, or had them take turns.

4-H Club work has been a boon to us in teaching kids to keep records, improve existing conditions, and how to upgrade a project, whether it be livestock or household chores. Rebecca and Maryanne learned the finer points of sewing their own clothes because they wanted to wear them; but pleasing the leader and receiving a blue ribbon helped them go the extra mile. Same with the boys with their hogs or sheep or rabbits.

The girls groomed their horses better in 4-H than on their own. Parents often are too close to their own children to expect the standards of excellence an outsider can challenge the child to achieve. I have often joked that 4-H is great for PARENTS! When our children are parents they will better understand the record-keeping, grooming, and getting ready for the shows and will be intelligently helpful to their children. I've been a 4-H leader and know the heartbreak of a child who had no cooperation at home.

We have believed in discipline all these years when permissiveness was running rampant in our world. We expected our children to do their chores before watching TV or reading a book. There's no time like now to get work done. It puts the pleasure in relaxing.

Studies must come early in the evening. We have exceptions for good reasons. No rule is ironclad, but to stretch it too often is to destroy it. Ralph always helped the children with math and the sciences while I helped with spelling, reading, and writing. We both supplied encouragement.

I have begun to understand a most important lesson after being exposed to it for twenty-eight years. A mother's work is made up of little things that have to be done right now.

I have to stop to put the beef in the pressure cooker with the chopped vegetables so it will be ready for dinner. The men want to eat reasonably near noon. Today, there's Mickey, Paul, Jon, Ralph, David, Julie and I. The biscuits can be popped into the oven after I do the chicken chores.

Now, let's see, where was I with making haste to write this book? Oh, yes, the childhood years. Oops, there's someone at the door. Our little Cambodian refugee girl wants to borrow the snow shovel.

This is Tuesday morning and I always type the family letter before the mailman goes so they receive it Thursday, near midweek. I make four copies because I care deeply about our children living away from home and about my mother. I do this chore to keep them in touch with little things that have happened here through the week.

Back to the book. But this is the first of the month. There are bills to pay, and how about the church paper? Better call and see if there's room for the missionary news. I'll type it quickly and run into the church office with it.

Better call Sandy and ask about the Thrift Boutique that we hope to reopen in the vacant store downtown. No, the line is busy. Now, here's Jon carrying in wood. Maybe I can get him to bucket feed the calf for me. Yesterday he did all my chores, but that was because it was a holiday and I was cleaning house for a buffet supper after the young people's sledding party on the hills. Funny how that made all the difference in his willingness; not that he's an unwilling boy, you understand.

That reminds me, I must make a dental appointment for Jonathan because he said it felt like there was a cavity when he brushed his teeth last night. That does it. I won't get any more typing done before noon.

A mother's work is designed so that she is always available for her family's needs. There are many things she can do with her time, but all these must give way to the necessities. When the baby is crying the most important thing is to change his diaper and feed him, then get back to whatever was underway. Mothers understand that the trivia in life involving family is important. Our lives seem centered in my kitchen. I talk with Ralph when he needs to think through decisions. I heard the boy-girl problems Paul had. Jon needs to be reminded to stick to that craft project till it's done. Then there's homework spread on the kitchen table at night.

Yet some people debate the need of mother in the home during these formative years?

I think about Jennifer, our granddaughter, who had a hard case of measles. The doctor suggested she go to the hospital because her mother, seven months pregnant, might not be able to take care of her. Sandy insisted she could, and she did nurse her through the worst. She said Jenny mostly wanted to be held and rocked so she just let the work go and sat and held her, soothing her aching eyes and comforting the little body against her own.

Thank God Sandy wants to stay home and take care of her children. If young mothers like her want government nurseries for their children while they go out into the world and pursue their own interests, think how children might become confused by workers who don't know how to love them, who might push them away when they wanted to be cuddled. This could easily prevent a well-rounded personality from developing.

God knew that a child needs a mother, father, brothers, sisters, grandparents, and neighbors when He ordained families. Who'd have ever thought the family would be an endangered species? We have columns, committees, and convocations on saving the family, but until both mother and father give up self-centeredness to work for the good of the whole family it will be in jeopardy.

In their younger years our children spent many fun-filled hours at the kitchen table cutting, pasting, modeling toy animals, and creating masterpieces in finger paint. They chattered contentedly while pots steamed and the oven warmed the room with the delightful aroma of supper baking.

Timothy generously shared his big "cookies" made with Homemade Modeling Clay at our kitchen table "nursery school."

I was unmarried and working out West when Luberta Jones gave me these recipes which I later used in my "kindergarten" when the children were small. Her Homemade Modeling Clay recipe is good.

Homemade Modeling Clay

1 cup flour
½ cup salt
3 teaspoons alum
food coloring
water

Mix ingredients as for dough and knead to consistency of clay. Be careful, it gets wetter as you knead. One can make large beads for stringing. Form beads, dry for several days before playing with them and store in a dry jar.

She also gave a recipe for finger paint that is almost as good as you can buy.

Finger Paint

¾ cup laundry starch mixed
      with cold water to dissolve
1½ cups soap flakes
1 quart boiling water
food coloring

Pour starch mixture into the quart of boiling water and stir until thickened. When slightly cool add soap flakes, stir well. Divide into 3 or 4 parts and place in small containers. Add food coloring to each. Use on glazed paper wet on both sides. Shelf paper will work.

Paste

In the outback country you may need paste and cannot get to town. Take 1 cup flour, 3 cups water, 1 teaspoon soda (to keep paste from souring). Prepare as for starch and boil 5 minutes. Add wintergreen flavor for a more commercial product.

Illinois Modeling Clay

Some people make modeling clay from another recipe I used in school.

1½ cups flour
½ cup salt
½ cup lukewarm water with food color
    added
1½ tablespoons vegetable oil

Knead till smooth. It may take a little more water.

Ice Cube Candles

Rebecca wanted me to include the recipe for ice cube candles which she and Maryanne used to make. They are simple for little children to do. It involves melting wax or paraffin in a double boiler, placing a string or candle wicking weighted through the middle of the cardboard carton you are using for a candle mold. Then just before pouring the wax, put cubes of ice partially crushed into the container and pour melted wax over them. It will provide a novel candle with myriad holes where the ice cubes were. Cut away cardboard carton after wax has hardened.

Natural Remedies

Since I was a little girl I have heard Grandma Bandelier talk about remedies that were good for about everything. Mother has told me many. Honey and vinegar for a sore throat eases it like nothing else can do unless it would be honey and lemon juice. Of course, that is cider vinegar. It is a mild purgative also.

Grandma and Grandpa Bandelier traveled with us when my parents and I went on vacation trips. I remember Grandpa's box of soda in the glove compartment and how he talked about it sweetening his stomach when the restaurant food didn't agree with him. He lived to be ninety-six years old. I would recommend it for anybody who has stomach problems.

Grandma carried in her purse a bottle of camphorated oil for the rheumatism she had. It was the beginning of my respect for it. Mother used it faithfully for sinus pains and headaches. In fact we were discussing it the other day, comparing it to anointing the head with oil and Biblical customs of pouring oil and vinegar on wounds. It helps with wintertime colds, dry nasal lining, cold sores, and, as an inhalant, soothes air passages.

Just recently I began to respect the cleansing value of salt. It would be a rude way to cleanse a wound, but it works. Mother's friend, Aunt Kate, told her a new use for mustard last winter when Kate was sick and needed a vomiting remedy. Cornstarch for galls has been used ever since horses had sore necks from rubbing horse collars. Now it is put to use in summertime for underarm gall. Ralph uses it and also takes salt tablets for water loss from profuse sweating. Factories issue their employees salt tablets on jobs where the heat is intense. Now, we use cornstarch on babies' bottoms when the powder can is empty. It works!

When the children come in from picking berries among the poison ivy we reach for the Fels Naptha soap. That natural soap is good for more than cleaning dirty clothes. Alum is in my cupboard for more than pickling recipes. The boys put it on canker sores in their mouths.

It is amazing how necessary the natural remedies have become in our family.

If you want to feel young and foolish again, give your attention to those knowlegeable folk who recognize every field plant and herb. In the last year I have been learning to recognize by name the plants I grew up with; Mother always said I grew like a weed. My ignorance was profound. I've always had a suspicion that everything is put here on earth for a purpose. I'm learning at last.

On recent prairie plant tours, a plant specialist identified plants for us. We took notes furiously and had our appetites whetted. After that a reader friend sent a large box of informative books, among which were herb identification cards in color, telling in plain English what each is good for.

It was a revelation to me to learn a good reason for wild carrot (which you may call Queen Anne's Lace) that haunts roadsides and field corners. It can help with liver, kidney, and bladder problems. Even the green cornsilk from our fields is a diuretic, demulcent, and milk stimulant for nursing mothers!

Mullein, those velvety leaved plants in the timber with regal flowered spikes, are helpful for diarrhea, washing open sores, toothache, and relief of other pains.

The pesky chickweed that grows at the doorstep and in our gardens is soothing and healing for any part of the body from raw sores to old ulcers. The root of milkweed is good for rheumatism, bowel and kidney trouble, asthma, stomach complaints, headaches, flu, and gallstones. What a wonderful weed!

I am in awe of a Creator who put together a universe that has in it a use for even the lowliest of weeds. They plague us and keep coming back when we pull, cut, or otherwise destroy them as if saying "Here I am am, use me and see how helpful I can be for your human frailties."

Epilogue

A Beautiful Day in Winter

Oh, what a beautiful day! I have accomplished a lot of homework and the book is finally finished. I feel just like Henry Van Dyke's The Other Wiseman, who was fully prepared to lay his precious gifts at the Lord's feet, but spent a lifetime being detoured into helping the needy, the hurting, the slaves, and the dying, on the way. However, in his search he learned what is important in life.

When I told a young visitor that I didn't know where I would rather be than here at home, feeding Paul's bottle lambs and all the other human lambs that come into my kitchen, I really meant it. I know I would grow impatient at any job away from home, thinking about all the things here. Right here in my own kitchen, the variety is exhilarating!

Some people look at it in a different way. They say that drudgery is deadening, or the sameness of every day drives them up a wall. They say the trouble with housekeeping is that it's so daily.

Personally, a desk job would be more deadening for me. I get enough desk work doing Ralph's bookkeeping and being his private secretary. I cannot get bored with the same faces when five, ten, or fifteen people traipse through my kitchen.

Today was a good example. Technically, we are snowbound with no school. Jon got up with two degrees of fever and I tried to make him comfortable, feeding him liquids for his cold. The two Cambodian refugee children who live on our farm thought there was school because they don't speak English yet and couldn't have understood the radio announcements that schools were closed and bus routes suspended. They came over ready for school, so I took them into the living room and tuned in Captain Kangaroo and Sesame Street while I fed Paul's lambs, did morning chores, and answered telephone calls about the postponed homemaker meeting that was to have been here today.

After the two hours of television Jon went back to bed and I had school for the two soft-spoken, smiling eager children. I felt it was a privilege to have a glimpse into their learning processes. Jon had reminded me that the boy was having trouble with subtracting double numerals. We checked that out, did some large multiplication and found they couldn't yet keep their columns straight. I showed them how to do it, then reviewed their picture dictionary. When we came upon "candy" I opened the container sitting on the table and let them taste it.

By that time the ham and beans were done and it was time to make the cornbread. I had to substitute soda because we've been snowbound and were out of baking powder. Noon hour was pleasant. Jon dressed and came downstairs thirsty. After an aspirin to kill his headache he wanted to talk. David and his wife Julie who came over to visit, fed the two little lambs in the utility room for me. I examined the coffeemaker after I poured the last cup for Ralph and unplugged it for the repairman. We chatted about farm finances, a very important subject these days. Ralph had wanted to ship some cattle last night and David had wanted to ship hogs tonight, but the blizzard stopped all that.

This afternoon Ralph went to help dig out the neighbor's machinery caught under a fallen roof when the snow got too heavy. We needed to cut wood for our fireplace and shop stove, but Ralph has a strong feeling of neighborliness.

189

I did the sheep chores, fed the chickens, cats, ducks, baby lambs, and bucket calf. Then I delivered a few groceries to the Cambodian refugees in the house across the lane. They need attention every day. I took eggs and showed the mother of the family how to make tuna meat patties and fried a few to give them a sample taste. She showed me a box of gelatine and wondered what to do with the powdery stuff. It was a puzzle to her. I boiled water, got her green bowl and let her stir the gelatine. Then I opened a can of peaches, drained the cool juice into the bowl and let some of the fruit slip in. I stirred in a few miniature marshmallows and gave them a taste. She smiled and called the children to come and try it. The surprise on their faces repaid me for the time it had taken from my busy day.

I had my hood and coat on ready to walk out when I saw they needed to be shown how to take a hot pad off the looper loom. Then I waved goodby out the door, realizing it was already 4:15 and I had to check on Jonathan. David stopped me enroute to the house to give me another lamb that was sick. He had given it penicillin and vitamin shots. He asked me to take the syringe to the sheep shed and give the two new lambs shots. I got into the house, took off my coat and boots and heard these lambs calling for more food.

It's a busy circle. It's not a vicious one, but a loving one, if prepared with prayer each morning. I trust the Lord to guide my steps to the most important things to do.

One of my New Year's resolutions had been to have fried potatoes more often for Ralph and Jon, so I began to peel potatoes for supper. The radio reported more snow on the way and no school for tomorrow. Maybe that would enable me to catch up on the jobs that I had intended to do today. It was better to have taken all the side roads than to have sat at my typewriter wondering what to write about. Now my fingers are ready to fly across the keys.

Supper is finished and dishes are done. I think I will have a nice quiet evening of reading after I have given Jonathan his medicine. Ralph is reading, too. But, wait, Jonathan wants to play dominoes. We have just learned to play and they are fun. Another evening gone and time to go out and check the livestock.

Ask any cook—washing dishes is the inevitable aftermath of mealmaking. Tired though I might be, I can approach this task with a light heart knowing that Ralph, the children, the many visitors, have enjoyed a warm, nourishing meal cooked by me from the bounty of our land.

Ralph and I walk out into the winter night to fire up the shop stove, check the sheep shed, and see that all the farmstead is tucked in. There is security about the glow of the heat lamps, like somebody keeping watch on the job.

We are just about to turn toward the house when Ralph steers me up the hill. The moonlight is diffused through lightly falling snow; horses whinney to us; the dog is alert for sport. She is used to going out late at night with Ralph to tree a coon or get a possum sneaking in for a kill in the poultry shed.

Ralph wants me to see the new hog barn since the men have put hogs in it. Finally, after many delays, it is in use.

I am glad we went to see the new hog barn by moonlight. It is a quiet, peaceful walk. Now our day is done. We go to bed for deep sleep to be ready to get up with the dawn of another new day.

Recipe Index